River Rover Chronicles

JOYCE KRAMER

WESTBOW®
PRESS
A DIVISION OF THOMAS NELSON
& ZONDERVAN

WestBow Press books may be ordered through booksellers or by contacting:

WestBow Press
A Division of Thomas Nelson & Zondervan
1663 Liberty Drive
Bloomington, IN 47403
www.westbowpress.com
1 (866) 928-1240

Because of the dynamic nature of the Internet, any web addresses or
links contained in this book may have changed since publication and
may no longer be valid. The views expressed in this work are solely those
of the author and do not necessarily reflect the views of the publisher,
and the publisher hereby disclaims any responsibility for them.

Any people depicted in stock imagery provided by Thinkstock are models,
and such images are being used for illustrative purposes only.
Certain stock imagery © Thinkstock.

ISBN: 978-1-4908-2963-0 (sc)
ISBN: 978-1-4908-2965-4 (hc)
ISBN: 978-1-4908-2964-7 (e)

Library of Congress Control Number: 2014904805

Printed in the United States of America.

WestBow Press rev. date: 03/14/2014

CONTENTS

GETTING TO KNOW THE FLINT RIVER

GETTING TO KNOW THE CHATTAHOOCHEE RIVER

GETTING TO KNOW SPRING CREEK

CHARIOTS OF FIRE - THE STEAMBOATS

A GUIDE TO FUN ON LAKE SEMINOLE

LAKE SEMINOLE SERVICES

LIST OF LANDINGS

DEDICATION

This book may not have happened if it weren't for the kindness and support from my readers and friends. Most of all, it was the encouragement from my late husband, Dale, that gave me the courage to do this. He took me wherever I wanted to go and explore. He encouraged me to keep writing - writing - writing. I truly miss him.

INTRODUCTION

All of the history, all of the mystery, all of the beauty, it is here, at Lake Seminole. The beauty is easy to see. However, the history and the mystery are harder to find. Even though the waters of Lake Seminole, the Flint and Chattahoochee Rivers and Spring Creek, shimmer just like diamonds in the sun, they all have their secrets. Millions of years ago, this area was very different from what it is today. There are all sorts of clandestine happenings hiding beneath the warm, calm surface of the lake and her rivers and streams.

Before history was recorded, civilization in the form of prehistoric Indians called this bountiful place home. They wandered through the area making camps, hunting and fishing all around the rivers. They build mounds to bury their dead, leaving behind evidence of their footsteps.

It is intriguing, knowing that under all that water people lived, loved and died. Sadly, their mysteries are now buried with them, silenced by the backed up waters that made Lake Seminole. However, in this book, I will attempt to expose some of these stories and place them in the sunlight. I will share stories of important happenings. Some are documented facts. Others are based in fact but dressed in legends. They were shared from generation to generation over a campfire and told on the front porch swing.

Then, after the spirits are freed from the confines of the lake, rivers and springs, I will acquaint you with the modern version of Lake Seminole, whose waters are so inviting. Teaming with fish, providing a home for birds and reptiles alike, they also supply the ingredients for fun. Sportsmen find paradise. Family and friends find fellowship. Couples find romance and children discover the wonders of nature. Yes, everything that God created for us to enjoy, is right here.

I have gathered together a list of landings which tells what facilities are offered at Lake Seminole. Included too, are the services along the rivers with a description of how to get there by boat or vehicle. Also, there is a list of where you can find gas and diesel to fuel your boat and restaurants to fuel your tummy. If the need arises, there is a list of marine repair shops, both engine and hull.

Armed with all of this information, you should have a most enriching adventure and enjoyable stay.

TRUE STORIES OF WILD TIMES

There Was Life On The Rivers Before Cell Phones

Today's life in southwest Georgia is so very different from that led by the original pioneers. Residents are polite, easy going and always ready to help friends and neighbors when the need arises. However, the early pioneer was not able to display these mannerisms. Life was very hard and neighbors were unpredictable and sometimes violent. This was due mostly to the fact that one side of the Flint and one side of the Chattahoochee was occupied by farmers, but the banks on the other side were populated by hostile Indians and thieves. While most men wanted to live in peace, they had to contend with a lawless element. Living under these conditions, manners were the least of everyone's worries.

One famous lawless area in the late 1700s, and early 1800s, was a wild looking village referred to as Sodom, which was across the Chattahoochee River on the Alabama side, just south of Columbus, Georgia. Consisting of scattered shacks on the edge of the forest, it was populated by notorious outlaws, murderers and thieves along with renegade Indians from all over. It was a rare day when no one was murdered or beaten there. People whose homes were in the surrounding woods were terrified and were afraid not to allow these outlaws to use their village as a hiding place.

The bad guys did not stay in what they considered their territory. At night, they would cross the river and rob and murder in established towns along the banks of the Chattahoochee. The peace loving citizens were not only attacked in the streets and woods, but in their own homes as well. They tried to get protection from the local law enforcement. They tried to get justice for what was being done. However, because the outlaws lived across the river in what was considered Indian territory, they could not be arrested. Living under these conditions, people felt insecure. Therefore, everyone carried a gun for personal protection and that of their families.

With life this hard, it is not surprising that the citizens of towns were as tough as those who lived in outlying areas and in the notorious villages across the rivers. People longed for an end to the violence and wanted order to be restored. They wanted a peaceful and tranquil life. However, in these most remote settlements, for this to happen, it was going to take a while.

The area of the Apalachicola River was another very wild frontier and also the scene of brutal murders. One notorious happening occurred in April of 1830. Two men were cutting wood to sell to the steamboats that were on their way down river. This was the business of a man named Samuel Price. Needing help, he hired a man called Field. On Friday, April 25, the men decided that this would be a day off for them and they settled down to drink whiskey and gamble at cards.

As the day progressed, the men began to feel the effects of the whiskey. A quarrel began about who owned a particular canoe. It apparently was lost in the card game. The loser felt that he was cheated.

Price, who was the actual owner, was determined to destroy the canoe rather than let Field have it. So, taking up an axe, he began to hack the boat apart. Seeing this, Field reportedly went into their shack and grabbed up a double barreled shotgun. He fired a load of buckshot into Price's chest, killing him. As was the custom, he buried him on the side of the river.

A couple of days later, Field arrived in Apalachicola, Florida, and surrendered himself to the authorities. He was put in jail, but after that no one knows what happened to him.

Owners and captains of steamboats did not always see eye to eye either. One had the priority of making money and the other had the priority of getting the steamboat safely to its destination. Sometimes this caused a fatal difference of opinion. One such fight over goals took place on board the steamboat, *Reindeer*.

In early November, 1836, at the Depot Creek tributary just down from Columbus, Georgia, a violent exchange took place between one of the steamboat owners, Mr. Victory, and the captain of the boat, Mr. Shaw. There was a meeting scheduled for this day. Both men had clashed before and knew that there would be a confrontation. Therefore, both came to the meeting armed.

They approached their problem with no spirit of give and take. As heated words were exchanged, Mr. Victory wanted Mr. Shaw to give up his position as captain on the *Reindeer*. The men drew their guns. Shaw was shot twice and Victory once.

No one expected either to live. However, after several days, both men began to recover. It is not known what happened to them after this.

This hard way of life spread to the steamboat, *Uchee*. It was in late September, 1838, and the *Uchee* was heavily loaded with freight. She was headed up to Columbus when she struck a snag and sank about 20 miles from her destination.

Captain Charles Klink wanted to save as much of his cargo as he could. He also wanted to lighten the boat in the hopes that it then would float up and off of the snag. To accomplish this, he ordered his deckhands to work twice as hard as they were used to.

Most of the men began unloading the boat but one refused. He grabbed a large log, cut for feeding the fire in the boiler, and went for the captain. The captain feared a mutiny and thus feared for his life. He drew his pistol and fired on the worker, killing him.

Once in Columbus, Captain Klink reported to the military government. He was completely cleared of charges. Captain Klink did not charge the other workers with mutiny.

The rivers were a hard place way back when. Who knows how many people found their final resting place to be along the river banks.

Revenge - Indian Attacks On Families And Steamboats

When it came to traveling the river system, the Creek and Seminole Indian Wars caused real fear. When going from Columbus, Georgia, to Chattahoochee, Florida, aboard a steamboat, passengers were very much aware that at any time and at any place on the river, one might encounter Indians.

Sometimes settlers fleeing from the Indian threat could be seen running along the river banks, their wagons loaded with all of the belongings that they could carry, fleeing for their very lives.

There were many instances where the conflicts with the Indians were brought close to home. One such happening was in early May of 1839. Some 15 or 20 Creek Indians attacked the settlement of Estiffanulga on the Apalachicola River as well as the one at Ricco's Bluff, also on the Apalachicola River. Involved in these assaults were the Roberts family and the Smith family.

At Estiffanulga, the Indians burned the Roberts' home and killed their little boy. Mr. Roberts was wounded but he and his wife and their farm hand, Aldrich, escaped along with their other four children.

The other attack that took place that day was at the home of Nathan Smith on Ricco's Bluff and resulted in a massacre. Nathan Smith's three children, a neighbor Mrs. Richards and her five children, along with a man named White were all murdered. Smith, his wife, another woman and two men escaped.

All in all, some 15 refugees from attacks on this day, carefully made their way along the river banks, hiding in the dense undergrowth and behind the massive trees. Gratefully, the small party heard a steamboat coming through the Narrows, about seven miles north of Fort Gadsden. It was the mail boat, *Commerce*, making her way down to Apalachicola, Florida. The refugees waved her down. What a welcome site that riverboat was! As she slowed to pick them up, the Indians were spotted along the river banks, not far from where the scared group had been.

A couple of days later, what had happened to these two families then happened to another one. A white family which arrived in Apalachicola, stated that their house, which sat on the bank opposite Blountstown, had been attacked and burned by a party of 30 or so Indians, perhaps the same group that attacked the others.

This family too, fled for their lives after seeing all that they had worked so hard for, their house and crops, being destroyed and being helpless to do anything to stop it. They had trekked southward, down river until they had reached the safety of the city.

Next, the marauding, hostile Indians seemed determined to take over a steamboat. They must have figured that in doing this it would surely cause fear in the white settlers. They may even have felt that this would slow down the amount of people coming to settle the river areas.

A huge effort by the Indians to capture a steamboat came in June of 1840, when they attacked the *Irwinton*. She was up bound to Columbus, Georgia, with 15 passengers, three of which were ladies. Just below the town of Irwinton, the steamboat was fired upon from both shores. A volley killed the cabin boy, John Gill of Pittsburg. So fierce was the fighting that some of the bullets passed clear through the cabin. However, the passengers were smart enough to lay down flat on the floor. Joined by the pilots, no one was injured.

Meanwhile, below the decks of the *Irwinton*, her engineer was firing up her boilers. At this time, the steamboat was towing a heavily loaded barge alongside. Some 11 Indians in a canoe attempted to board this barge with three of them jumping onto it. This action caused their canoe to capsize throwing the other eight Indians overboard. These men then floated downstream, away from the battle to capture the *Irwinton*.

The three Indians that were left, then went from the barge to the steamboat. Two of them were killed by the *Irwinton's* mate and engineer, who knocked them down by hitting them with one of the huge wrenches used to work on the boilers. They then threw the enemy into the paddle wheel house where they were torn to pieces.

The lone remaining Indian, presumably the leader, did not realize what had happened and thought the other two were behind him. He entered the cabin and sat down at the head of the table. A passenger, grabbed a chair for defense and threw this at the surprised Indian. A stout Georgia man of about 50, then grabbed the Indian wrapping massive arms around him from behind. He tried to force him out of the cabin, away from the other passengers but he was not able to do this. At this time, one of the riverboat men came in. He stabbed the Indian in the stomach and proceeded to throw him into the deadly paddle wheel.

In the spring of 1841, the steamboats and the Indians were once again in the news as the Indians were still trying to hijack one. At the town of Irwinton, a log fort was hastily constructed for defense but fortunately, no attacks came and it was never used.

However, it was different in Roanoke, Georgia, just south of Columbus. On May 20, 1840, the tiny town was raided by Indians and completely destroyed. The steamboat, *Georgian*, was at the town dock. It had to get up steam quickly by stoking the furnaces with bacon and lard to keep the Indian pirates away. During this battle at Roanoke, the *Georgian* was fired upon several times while trying to leave. She did get underway without a loss of life.

Silt That Covered The Unknown - West Bank Of Lake Seminole

An area of the rivers that was the scene of a lot of human inhabitance was on the very high bank, on the western side of the Chattahoochee River, near the place that is now known as the West Bank Overlook. This bank was a natural levee formed by the Chattahoochee River which, through the centuries, kept depositing its soil there, especially during floods. No one guessed what treasure lay below this collection of silt.

The history behind the West Bank was first discovered during the excavation that took place in 1948, before the Woodruff Dam was built. The work began by laying out the dig in squares. The teams worked carefully, only digging four inches at a time. In a painstaking manner, the layers of soil were gently removed.

Upon reaching the depth of two feet, a large village site was uncovered. Great excitement spread amongst the teams. They had found the remains of over 30 post holes which had served as columns for log houses which made up the old village.

Then came the unearthing of numerous fire pits still containing the bones of animals and mussel shells. There were chunks of charcoal and even charred corn cobs uncovered as well. All in all, thousands of artifacts were discovered over the wide village area. When subjected to radio carbon dating, a probable date of 1400 AD, was discovered. It is believed that this was a thriving Indian community which existed around the time the Spaniards first arrived here.

Not yet satisfied, the archeologists decided to dig even deeper. Their patience was rewarded when they found artifacts of a period existing somewhere around 300 BC to 100 BC.

Now the adrenaline was really rushing. With all of these exciting finds, the team wanted to keep digging. Continuing on at four inches at a time and using small brushes and spoons for shovels, they kept to the task at hand. They went through several more feet of river silt. Again, their patience was rewarded when they found more evidence of human occupation. This time the pottery shards were thick. Some were decorated with intricate details.

Along with the pottery were some 60 stone tools as well as charred nuts, deer bones and turtle shells. This evidence showed that there was a small group of Indians who must have been hunters and fishermen and who lived there around the year 1200 BC!

Still working on hunches fed by other evidence found around the West Bank Overlook area, they continued digging, unearthing the past as they went. Finally, several more feet down, they came to what was to be the last evidence of life. This was 14 feet below the modern surface. Here they continued to find pottery shards that were described as being of the Pre-Ceramic Period which dated them to existing before 2000 BC or much earlier!

Finding so many artifacts was incredible! This one location, was home to four different civilizations, each from a different time period, all on top of each other. Although it can't be proved because our climate hastens decay, perhaps the first man to walk the Overlook was a wandering Paleo-Indian hunter from some 6000 years ago.

All the artifacts which were removed were treated carefully. They were examined, identified and ultimately became exhibits in the Smithsonian Institute.

Strange Stories About Red Bluff

Many areas have their colorful places, full of legends and stories. They add life to the fabric of the history. There are many such areas in southwest Georgia. One of these is near Bainbridge, along the Newton Road that winds its way next to the Flint River, off an extension of Spring Creek Road. About seven miles north of Bainbridge, it is called Red Bluff.

There is a small, pull off on the side of the road here, where once the vivid, red clay cliffs were visible. However now, the area is well overgrown, thick with underbrush.

The history here spreads out to more than Bainbridge. It goes all the way up to New York City. During the building of the Brooklyn Bridge many sturdy, heavy timbers were needed. The gigantic girth of our area pines was just perfect for this project.

The construction of the Brooklyn Bridge began in 1868. When completed in 1883, it connected Brooklyn and Manhattan. The Carl Haddon Company was contracted to cut and shape the lumber. Doing this required strength and special skills when using the broad axe. Southwest Georgia had many talented lumbermen who could do this work.

Local lumber companies were also involved. Flint River Lumber Company, E. Swindell Company and Stewart Lumber Company, all helped with this construction.

Many pines were cut, then floated down the Flint to the Apalachicola River and then on to the port of Apalachicola, Florida. Here, they were loaded on ships and taken up to New York City.

Taking these huge logs down river required special skills. Raft men were trained in how to bring these logs down stream. They needed to use long poles called sweeps to navigate the huge timbers around river bends. The raft men also had to avoid steamboats which not only meant not hitting them but also maneuvering their wakes.

This local timber was also used to build a wooden bridge that spanned the Flint River just up from the now Highway 84 bridge.

Most of the stories told of Red Bluff show the independent spirit that the South is famous for. The number one story shared tells of a happening during the Great Depression. Many people in the area were hit hard by this financial disaster.

Trying to fight back and in frustration at the situation, when the bank threatened to take away their cars and trucks, they were driven to Red Bluff and shoved over the cliff into the deep water below. However, some did not make it down the cliff and became hung up on the side. Eventually, the banks had to hire people to go and retrieve the vehicles from the water and the river bank. However, they were not able to get all of them and some are still in their watery graves.

Another aspect of the area that got everyone thinking was where the name Red Bluff came from. Most thought that it was because of the color of the clay. However, some long time residents heard stories from their grandparents, which were in turn told to them by their grandparents about how Red Bluff got its name.

Somewhere back in time, after the Civil War, some Georgia men and a young drummer boy banded together to walk home. As they made their journey through the woods, they were ever watchful for snakes and wild animals. For a while, everything went well. However, they began to feel they were being stalked. The only defense they had were knives and each other.

The dense underbrush and black pine forests became more and more foreboding. The men heard noises. Some smelled a terrible stench. Others saw movement around them. Then, on a cold, foggy night while camped at what is now Red Bluff, they encountered the phantom, the largest bear anyone had ever seen.

They all fought valiantly, but the beast was too much for them. As it tore and ripped at the men, the young boy escaped. He ran and ran until he found civilization at Bainbridge.

He brought help back but all were dead. The ground was soaked red with their blood, thus, Red Bluff.

Southwest Georgia's Own Ghost Town-Chevertown

Ghost town. Just the very words bring to mind images of hauntings and of the people who lived, laughed and loved in a certain area but are now restless spirits. Also, when the words "ghost town" are said, most people think of the Old West. However, Georgia has her share of these once bustling places that are now the source of legends. One of these is Chevertown. However, it has a somewhat different claim to fame than most of the local, forgotten towns. Not only is it known because of its being constantly destroyed by floods but because it was the site of a prison.

Chevertown was located in what is now Baker County, which was formed from Early County in 1825. Most of Baker County's history is about the floods. Here, the usually tame Flint River would occasionally explode out of the confines of its banks and inundate all that is around it. Being located near the mouth of Itchawaynichawa Creek, which drains into the Flint River, flooding would happen quite often to Chevertown.

Low water, too, created its own set of problems. Chevertown needed the water to be somewhat high so that the steamboats could get up to the landing. Most of the time, it was accessible. However, sometimes riverboats would get up there, but were not able to float back down. Then, they would dump their cargo on shore. Being lighter, they were setting up higher in the water and could go back down river. When the boats would leave, the residents would go to the landing site and take whatever they needed from the cargo left behind there.

However, floods brought the most devastation. One particular tragedy is still talked about. It involved the Alderman family. Sarah Martin Adams Alderman was the granddaughter of an original settler, James Martin who came to what became Chevertown from South Carolina.

After her husband passed on, Sarah decided to continue to run the family business, a ferry across the Flint River. During one particularly rough water day in 1828, tragedy struck this family. Sarah's young son, Choice Hall Adams, and two helpers drowned while trying to secure the wildly pitching ferry.

Despite the flooding, Chevertown hung on and became an official town in the early 1870s. It was named for William Chever who, at the age of 28, became mayor of Albany, Georgia. Chevertown prospered for 50 years mainly because of the turpentine industry. The high point in population was in the 1880s, when approximately 100 families inhabited the town.

In 1886, the town had seven mercantile stores, a milliner, and grist mill. There was also a church, an academy, a blacksmith and post office, as well as a doctor and two saloons.

As the years passed, Chevertown developed into quite a bustling place. It became a prime area for the production and shipment of lumber and turpentine products. It also was the center for liquor distribution and fish scraps for fertilizer. These items caused numerous complaints from residents, those who were opposed to alcohol and those who could not stand the stench of rotting fish on hot summer days.

Perhaps the largest claim to fame for Chevertown was the fact that on October 3, 1898, a Misdemeanor Convict Camp, better known as the Chain Gang Camp, was established two miles from the town. This facility was jointly owned by Baker, Miller and Decatur Counties.

The prison came about because in 1898, the state of Georgia first attempted to prohibit the sale of liquor. Many did not agree. Thus there was a lot of trafficking in moonshine. This created a large influx of prisoners.

In the 1900 census, 47 prisoners were listed as turpentine laborers. The convicts in the Chain Gang Camp were leased as turpentine laborers to work in the vast pine forests of the area. The men were chained together for the walk through the woods to where they would be working that day. The main danger to these men were the rattlesnakes. They were abundant in these virgin forests. To help keep the snakes at bay, the men walked the same path each day making noise so the dangerous reptile would scurry away.

These men would carve the famous "cat faces" into the long leaf pines and then nail on the metal gutters that directed the turpentine into the pails which were attached to the tree and emptied daily.

There were very few paid employees at the prison. There was the warden, a few guards and a whipping boss.

There is some confusion as to if the prison was physically located in Baker County or Miller County. The misconceptions may have been caused due to the camp's proximity to the county line. Confusion may also have been caused by the 1900 census. In the population count, part of the 47 prisoners were listed in Baker County and the other part were listed in Miller County. Also, perhaps the land being owned by a man named Matt Miller caused confusion too. Also, some long time residents even deny that the camp existed. However, land records show that the prison was two miles below Chevertown, in Baker County.

As time went on, high water and flooding caused extreme havoc and did eventually destroy Chevertown. She lost her hold on to the land and nothing remains but the memories. However, if you know your way through the woods, you can walk to where the Flint River and the Itchawaynichawa Creek come together and try to imagine Chevertown.

Action On The Gator Banks

One thing I have noticed about the Chattahoochee River is that it is home to lots of alligators, seems like one a mile! I really don't know why this is. There is a lot of boat traffic. There aren't that many places where alligators can hide in the grasses. It must be because a gator can find a lot of food out there. Since gators are eating machines, they can be rough customers, especially when encountered out on the water while you are in a small boat.

The story comes to mind of the fisherman who fought off a gator that wanted his dog for a chew toy. Another story involves a giant crane that was dredging out the land near the shoreline. Ruthlessly, the metal bucket penetrated into the soft earth, which gave way and dislodged a gator nest. As the huge steel bucket descended again, momma gator attacked it. Savagely, she tried to eat this threat to her young.

Other lake residents tell of a 10 foot momma gator who had arranged herself in front of her nest, protecting it against any assault from a boat. She looked like a log, but this log had teeth!

Blue sky, calm water, a beautiful day. Two men were riding down the channel to Lake Seminole. They passed the place where the land reaches out toward the water, the place where momma gator had chosen to guard her nest. When the small, 14 foot craft came close, she raced off the bank and began chasing it. She started twisting, somewhat like a tornado, then stopped and pounded her tail on the surface of the water, preparing to deal a direct hit onto the noisy, shiny intruder that was a threat to her nest.

The men turned the boat and began to veer away from the angry gator. With her size and state of mind, she was a danger. They were relieved to be leaving her behind.

Here is another alligator story which is told over camp fires at Lake Seminole:

Desperately, he clung to the side of the small, wooden fishing boat. His wet, blue jeans and boots felt like giant stones, beckoning him to sink downwards into the black water of the pond. His heart was pounding hard. Blood pushed against his ear drums. He could barely hear the grunts from the alligators which were now surrounding him. Their red eyes showed like devil orbs as they peered out of the tall grasses.

During the day, the lake shone like a jewel in the Georgia sunshine. Not so on this horrible night. He had fished here a hundred times. His boat was big enough. His engine had always responded.

Suddenly, he heard splashes, felt ripples. Cold sweat dripped into his eyes. The realization came. The gators knew he was there. Oh God, how his arms ached as he clung to the boat.

What was that! A brush against his legs? Red eyes now circled him, pulsating the water with deadly tails. The adrenaline rush gave him the strength to try to climb onto the boat.

His attention changed to the sound of truck engines and headlights which now were piercing the blackness. Suddenly, boats hit the water and engines screamed as men shouted. The red eyes took on a fearful glow. They darted and scattered, looking for safety. The man was saved.

Of course, I am sure gators have stories about us too. Perhaps they go like this. Why did the human cross the swamp. We will never know, but we hope his friends come looking for him! Please pass the barbeque sauce.

LEGENDS TOLD ABOUT LAKE SEMINOLE

Jake And Marlow

An early morning boat ride amidst the fog and pale sun brings to mind a legend that longtime residents tell about our Lake Seminole. Be sure you have a light on when you read this.

The deep black of the pines and the low gray clouds floated overhead, soundless as they mingled with the opaque water on the horizon. Only certain milky white rays were allowed to penetrate and blend into this strange, heavy atmosphere which enveloped the small boat. Jake, was making his way through a dangerous passage which went from Sealy's Landing to the outer islands. It was rumored that here gargantuan size fish lived. They grew to be oversized because of the pure, crystal waters. It was also a favorite haunt for giant turtles and alligators of great size. Even giant snakes, from rattler to king, inhabited this overgrown, lush area.

Our boatman, Jake, was a local fisherman, a loner. He loved to fish in the very early morning amongst the stumps off Sealy's Landing. Jake was no stranger to these waters. At 84 years old, he had fished in the "old" Spring Creek before her virgin waters were tampered with. He had seen all of the changes brought on by the dam which caused the area to turn from land to water.

Now, Jake enjoyed the solitude of this time of the day and the sunrise reflecting on the water emphasizing the many stumps. This particular morning, here at the confluence of Spring Creek and the Flint River, something was different, not right. The air was too heavy. It was too hard to breathe. Jake didn't feel like staying out as long on the water as he had in the past. Something was making the hair on the back of his neck stick up.

He studied his small, well worn, aluminum boat as he made his way to the stern to the sometimes reliable motor. He was going to sit there and pilot his skiff over the inky black water.

Somehow, he felt he was not alone. He felt that he was being watched through the mist of early morning. Jake decided not to try to find these eyes nor to look back. He had heard that this could cause an attack. For sure he didn't want that. He had heard the legends, passed down from Indian times, about the huge turtles and giant gators. He had even seen these reptiles from a distance.

No one believed him. No one treated his story as true, for no one else had seen the turtle whose head was the size of a basketball or the gator whose eyes were some five feet from the tip of his nose.

Sure enough, Jake's son, Marlowe, did not believe his father when he told him about his feelings of being stalked. As the son listened to the story he laughed, "Foolish old man." He would prove him wrong.

Just before sunrise, he took his 22 foot boat with its 120 horsepower motor, out to his Dad's favorite fishing hole near Sealy's Landing. The fog hung low above the flat water. A thick rumble of thunder broke the heavy silence.

Nothing was biting and Marlowe surely didn't want to get wet, so he decided to pick up anchor and leave. This is when he saw it, a gator so huge that as it aggressively slapped its tail, it caused an enormous wave. The rocking took Marlowe off guard and thrust him on to the floor of the boat. With menacing quickness the gator circled the craft. As the gator stopped, it glared at Marlowe. This is when Marlowe made the mistake of glaring back. His angry brown eyes challenging the giant red eyes, which were the size of golf balls.

Before he could draw his last breath, Marlowe was in the gator's mouth. The last thing he saw was a turtle so huge that its mouth devoured his motor.

There are many boaters who stay away from this section of the waterways. Too many spooky happening. Even though man built a dam, drilled for oil so deep that salt water invades certain places, these animals may still call this section of the lake home.

Your Mother Will Love You, No Matter What

Some of us believe that when there is an event which takes away something, an event so big, so intense, that ghosts are left behind. For some of the residents of the lake area, the appearance of Lake Seminole was just such a happening. The flooding of the land for the lake was something that the inhabitants at the time believed would not happen. Communication was very poor at best. Lots of things which circulated by word of mouth were exaggerated or just not so. Still, the people couldn't believe that the government was taking away their land for this project. They couldn't believe that Spring Creek, Flint River and the Chattahoochee River could be harnessed. Therefore the building of the dam does come under the category of a monumental event.

Thus comes this story which tells of the power of love. It is about a mother and her son who lived in a small cabin, way out in the wilderness near where the Flint River and Chattahoochee River once came together.

The Woodruff Dam had been built and the water was now busy seeking its own natural level, a process which would take quite some time.

Try to imagine how much the landscape changed when the water rose. Low lying areas succumbed easily to the encroaching lake. However, even with all the planning and surveying, the ponds and islands which popped up overnight were a constant surprise. The trees were full of leaves then. This foliage obscured most of the area. It was easy to get lost, for going around one tree looked just like going around another.

At this time, the occupants of a little cabin, a mother and her son, found that their home, once on the mainland, was now on an island. The mother checked the cupboards and seen that they had run out of supplies. A trip to town was necessary. So her son could find his way back home, the mother promised she would leave the oil lamp on in the house like she had done so many times before.

When his shopping was finished, the son set out to make his way home. However, darkness came quickly as a storm came up. He worked his way toward what he believed was the site of his home and his mother. He had been out in the dark on the "big water" before. However, for some reason, this time the landscape wasn't as easy to follow as the young man had experienced in the past.

Then, slowly, the encroaching clouds brought big rain drops which began to pelt his shoulders and back. As he paddled quicker toward what he thought was his destination, a nasty current began to bring on churning waters from the Chattahoochee River. The mud and rain joined with the dark storm and the young man became very lost.

In the meantime, his mother was living up to her promise. As the sky became leaden, she lit the oil lamp which sat in the cabin window so it could guide her son home.

As the storm worsened, the concerned mother peered out the smoky glass of the cabin. She squinted her eyes, straining to see if she could see her son, paddling toward home. She imagined his homecoming. She'd made his favorite meal and she would pour him a large sweet tea.

Suddenly, she noticed a wall of muddy water, coming quite quickly in her direction from the Chattahoochee River. She gasped as the river, which seemed to be revolting against the binds which were placed upon it by all the dams, heaved toward her cabin on the tiny island.

As the wave approached, she prayed. She watched in horror as this water from the newly formed lake kept coming, encroaching upon her cabin. She then became resolved to what was to be her unexpected fate. She had no escape. She could not swim. She had no boat. So, as the water came closer and closer up the sides of the cabin and seeped under its door, the mother tended the light. She kept it burning in hopes that her son would see it. In hopes that he would come back in time and would rescue her.

However, as the water rose inside the tiny cabin and began to cover the meager furnishings, she gave up that hope. Chilled through to the bone, she filled the lamp for the last time and went to lie down in her bed. There she laid and prayed to the Lord to accept her soul as the cabin went under the relentless flow sending her into a cold, wet grave.

Whether her son ever found his way home is not known. However, it is said that when you are out on the lake, in the area between the burial mounds and the mouth of the Chattahoochee River, if you look down and focus your eyes on the murky bottom, you can still see the light from the cabin and the old woman looking out the window, waiting for the return of her son.

Encounter At The Devil's Playground

Lake Seminole, its rivers and the surrounding land are ideal places for hauntings. There are ancient civilizations which were flooded. Along with them went their secrets, now hiding from view. Many Indians lost their lives on the banks here and many steamboat men died and were buried in the woods nearby. Soldiers who fought in the Indian Wars, as well as the Civil War, have found their final resting place here, in southwest Georgia.

This is why one can encounter a paranormal being at any time and in any place around here. These ghosts want their stories to be told so that they can find rest or perhaps feel more at home. One channel in particular has more than its share of ghosts and that is the one that leads to the place that I call the Devil's Playground. It is here, on a beautiful sunny day, I unexpectedly ran into one of these restless spirits.

Looking back, it seems as though everything was trying to block my passage. I just did not heed the signs. This was to be an afternoon of exploring a shrouded waterway. I did not realize that on this boat ride, I would enter an unknown realm.

It started out happy, enjoying a beautiful day until the boat approached an uncharted channel. I had noticed it several times while on the way up the Chattahoochee River from Lake Seminole. I searched an old map of the area and found that at one time, it was charted and it still had the channel markers.

However, now most of the time, this area is inaccessible because of sand bars, fallen trees and thick water grasses. However, this day the grasses were down and the water was up.

The boat glinted in the hot Georgia sunshine as it went father inside the slough, totally unsuspecting of what the fate would be that day. The dead carcass of an alligator should have been a warning. It glistened, a slimy heap in the heat of the day. Its belly looked like a pale, white moon. Then, consumed by the wake, it was temporarily buried only to be resurrected again.

I began to recall tales of battles and massacres. I recalled some of the most interesting facts about what was ahead. Here, prehistoric burial mounds were discovered. Damp and decay had reduced all but two bodies, which were found lying cuddled together on charcoal, a pile of human fragments. People had lived here. These remains were their testament.

Also, discovered here were the remains from three Spanish missions started and abandoned around the late 1600s. There was also an Indian fort and the remains of an ancient home. They all shared this land throughout history.

Just then a giant fish jumped across the bow and brought me back to the present. The channel began to twist. Then it narrowed. Wild bundles of cattails and reeds began encroaching, trying to block the progress as they waved a warning. Lily pads sporting white blooms looked so deceptively innocent. More and more stumps began popping up helter skelter. The air became heavy, musty with the smell of something not quite alive.

Spanish moss hung like so many gray ropes from huge, black limbs. Then, they ended in what looked like a hangman's noose. Cypress knees broke through the water's surface, twisted and grotesque, like bones broken and knurled that had torn their way through skin.

Suddenly, the channel narrowed again and almost disappeared. The blue sky became black and ominous. Unexpectedly, a small lake opened up in front, only to disappear again in wild array. This was the end, a bowl of emerald green water surrounded by black smothering trees.

The boat slid over something. Then came a high pitched squeal, like a cry of pain. It filled the thick air. Cold sweat trickled down my back and dripped from my forehead into my eyes. Now, I was an unsuspecting traveler happening upon a fury from the past.

Again, I remembered the bones buried for centuries which had been taken from under the water their secrets exposed and placed out in the torturous sun. Now they wanted to extract revenge upon the intruder.

Dirt from the yellow banks began to swirl, causing the slough to become a desert in a storm. As I licked the sand from my lips, the large heavy cooler which sat on the floor of the boat, was sucked up into the swirling vortex. My life jacket was being tugged upon in the effort to rip it from my body. Swirl, swirl, I hung on to the boat for my very life.

Then, as mysteriously as it all began, all became silent. The boat was now resting upon the sandy shores of the slough, dumped there like a small child's toy when he was tired of it.

Tree limbs no longer twisted in pain. Dust no longer was thrown into the air to sting eyes and make breathing practically impossible. Still words would not come but were smothered by the thick green air and the tangle of underbrush and marsh grasses.

Slowly, senses returned and the ravenous rays from the summer sun took its place. Silently as a snake, the boat carved its way through the water, trying not to make a ripple, not to disturb further the fury of this force.

The motor droned and echoed in the enclosure and my mind prayed, "Please don't stop. *It* may be coming up behind," but, what was *it*?

As a blue heron croaked and glided across the channel, I made my way out onto the Chattahoochee River. Once again, the water seemed so bright so inviting, its surface warm and shiny. Whatever the threat was, it stayed silent for now. Once again, it was waiting amongst the shadows. For the water holds on to its secrets until the next unsuspecting victim floats by unawares that they are in the Devil's Playground.

HISTORY THAT SHAPED LAKE SEMINOLE

Holding Onto An Icon

Some places are just beguiling. They hold a fascination that cannot be explained. Within the confines of their walls are mysteries and memories of times long past. A large, yellow, concrete structure, quite aged, built across a modest, unassuming waterway called Spring Creek, is one such structure, the Spring Creek Powerhouse and Dam. Today, more than one hundred years since its construction, it continues to evoke a wide range of emotions from curiosity to amazement in residents and visitors alike.

This structure is more than just wood and mortar, much more. Within and without its yellow walls the feet of history have trod. Aside from its former usage as an electrical generation plant, the Spring Creek Powerhouse and Dam area has witnessed the activities of many families fishing, picnicking, romancing and enjoying the simple pleasures in life. Wonderful memories of family reunions and friendships which originated in this vicinity have persevered for generations.

When you cross over the bridge on Spring Creek Road and see this structure for the first time, it becomes a source of curiosity and intrigue. Questions, questions, questions, they just keep popping randomly. What is that building? How did it get there? Has it changed much? Who worked or resided there? This unique yellow building seems to hold a key that opens a walkway into history making you want to find out more about this structure of the past.

Today, there is no recorded document which indicates that anyone lived on or used this acreage prior to the construction of the Spring Creek Powerhouse and Dam. The first record of any official ownership appears in 1905, when a bank held the title to the property.

In August of 1919, the Bainbridge Power Company was formed. The directors of this company purchased the Spring Creek tract and quickly began construction of the dam. There was just enough fall in the flow of water in this vicinity to allow the generation of hydroelectric power via turbines and the power company officials took advantage of it. The powerhouse across Spring Creek went into operation in late 1920.

Unfortunately, the Bainbridge Power Company wasn't in business very long and the powerhouse changed hands several times. Then, on September 28, 1927, this facility and its transmission lines and power stations were sold yet again, this time to Georgia Power and Light Company. They operated the powerhouse for some thirty years, until in the late 1950s the Jim Woodruff Lock and Dam replaced it for electrical generation.

The type of construction used for the Spring Creek dam wall is called a rolled earth embankment. It was reinforced with timbers and stone and stretched east to west approximately 1,500 feet in length. At the west end of the earthen dam, there was a rock filled timber crib dam which angled southwest across the creek measuring 270 feet long. Another shorter, 120 foot rolled earth embankment extended southwest from the powerhouse. The impounded water behind the earthen and crib dams, is still known as Lake Decatur. The solid dam wall held firm for many years until the early 1950s, when the water began to break through.

The exterior of the powerhouse is still the original color of yellow from when it was constructed in 1919. Back then, this was a very popular color for industrial buildings. Now, most of the paint is a chalky yellow - white, where it has remained upon the concrete.

The structure is approximately 60 feet, 6 inches by 38 feet 8 inches in size. Erected with the best materials of that day, the Spring Creek Powerhouse and Dam was well built. Most of the workers were from the area and took pride in the construction of this landmark.

Walking out onto the concrete walkway on the north side of the building takes you back to the early years. This slab is worn from time, weather and the footsteps of the many people who came to fish and work there. Listening with the heart, one can hear the echoes of bygone voices as they discussed business, talked and laughed all on this well worn porch like structure.

A metal and wood walkway is on the northeast side, perched precariously over the moving waters of Spring Creek. A part of the original building, this walkway has rotted beyond repair. Numerous boards are missing, so it cannot be venture out on to. However, gazing down upon it, you can see the worn places on the thin metal bar where hundreds of fingers grasped the cold, hard surface.

Looking up, we notice another item from the past clinging to the building. It is a spotlight that is perched above the peeling wooden door on the water's side. Try to think of what it was like when it glowed in the darkness, its muted, golden shaft shining down on the impounded waters of Lake Decatur.

Back up on the land and closer to the entrance of the building, an old live oak tree spreads its branches out over the grassy meadow like a prehistoric beast. A breeze gently causes drapes of Spanish moss to sway. No doubt, when this building came into existence, that tree was there to greet those who entered this very door.

Just past this heavy wooden door, is a concrete stairway. Without any windows, there is thick darkness inside. Even though this is a brilliant sunlit day, a light is needed to continue on exploring the interior.

A switch is found and the darkness is pierced as overhead a dull light bulb flickers on, revealing the existence of a bare, oversized room. Its emptiness is punctuated only by a fireplace on the north wall. We have entered into the second floor of the now three story building.

The two large turbines which generated electricity were located on the floor below. The second floor, where we are, was designed as office and work space with a desk and files. The turbines were accessible through trap doors in this floor. Today, under normal conditions, the turbine floor is just barely above the level of the water in the creek and during rainy weather, this floor is submerged beneath the moving waters. This is because the Woodruff Dam drastically changed the dynamics of the water level in this area.

The third floor was not added until the late 1950s, when the facility was decommissioned and the powerhouse was remodeled. This floor came into existence when the very high ceiling of the second floor was altered enough to make another floor above it. Then, this new space was divided into a large great room and kitchen. Several bedrooms were partitioned off of the main room. These changes allowed this floor to be used as a fishing lodge, but this was just for a short time. It was also used for a while by the Department Of Natural Resources and the Fish & Wildlife Commission as a ranger station. Today, the Army Corps of Engineers is responsible for its upkeep. It has been deemed structurally sound and was "mothballed" to further preserve it.

Memories Of The Spring Creek Powerhouse And Dam

The story of the dam is often a subject in oral histories. Those who remember may have eyes clouded over by age, but the memories are crystal clear. Many remember their fathers working on the construction and leaving home for work at sunrise. Then they would walk down to the dam which in some cases was ten miles from their homes.

They remember how mules were put to work pulling away the trees and stumps left behind in what would shortly become Lake Decatur. Mules were also used to deposit dirt into low spots along the creek banks.

Now, imagine the whine of the turbines that would have been working below us. Hear the roar- slam of the water flowing forward and causing them to spin. Many area residents remember these sounds which were heard for miles as the powerhouse generated electricity for the cities of Bainbridge, Donalsonville, Brinson, Iron City and other surrounding areas.

A more recent memory involves a flood in the 1940s, which damaged the powerhouse. So high and powerful was the potent flow of the water in Spring Creek that it washed away the heavy iron gates which protected the turbines below the powerhouse. The flood and its resulting damage couldn't have occurred at a worse time either. For this was during World War II, a period when many items were being rationed and manufactured equipment was exceedingly difficult to obtain. There was only one logical course of action. The workers at the powerhouse would have to find these gates and reinstall them.

After the flood waters had subsided, the responsibility for the search for the gates required the services of someone who was an accomplished swimmer. This was Joe Nichols. Jumping in, he held his breath and submerged deep below the dam. He checked the hard, clay bottom, carefully searching for the heavy gates. Despite his efforts, Joe was unable to find them.

Through the years, many others have gone down into the cold water in search of the gates. Even when Lake Decatur was drained down so the dam wall could be dynamited, they were never found, their ultimate fate unknown.

Many times it was necessary for divers to check out the earthen wall. Back in those days, divers looked like those seen in the movie, *Voyage To The Bottom Of The Sea*. The diving helmet fitted over the man's head and then was screwed onto the suit.

The air pump which provided the life giving oxygen to the diver, looked like nothing more than a tin can. It was held by a man on land who pumped air into a rubber line by "squishing" the canister by hand.

A humorous story told by residents recalls a time when Joe Nichols and a fellow worker, Clayton Skipper, were to replace a piece of tin which had blown off the powerhouse roof during a storm.

The first challenge confronting the two men was the location of a ladder high enough to allow them to get onto the roof. After much searching, they finally found one.

The second challenge was presented when the men realized the slipperiness of this roof. If they fell off, it was a long, drop into the water below. After a bit of creative thinking, the two men came up with a solution. They would tie themselves together with a long rope which was wrapped around their waists on each end. This way, with the rope strung over the peak of the roof, they could counter balance each other. One man would work on one side of the roof, while the other took care of repairs on the opposite side.

As they walked precariously along the edge of the roof, Joe and Clayton joked back and forth to each other. "Don't let me down now! Hold on to me," they yelled, enjoying this little bit of humor and secure in their innovative thinking.

At one point during these repairs, Joe needed to nail a piece of tin in place. He was feeling along the side of the overhang, trying to find a rafter onto which he could nail the tin, when his hand suddenly skirted over a wasp nest. Instantly, he was horrified, and tried to flee to escape the painful stings of the insects.

Forgetting that he was attached to Clayton, Joe ran headlong across the roof, a bull moose charging for the safety of the ladder and the ground. In his hast to escape the wasps, Joe completely forgot that he was dragging Clayton along with him on the opposite side of the roof. Unaware of Joe's predicament with the wasps, Clayton suddenly found himself bouncing uncontrollably across the roof!

As with most things, there are memories of tragedies too. One in particular affected area residents for a long time. It happened sadly enough on Christmas Eve, in 1929.

As was sometimes the case in those days just as today, an alert came in that the electric wires were down from the poles in one area. Upon receiving notice of the emergency, three men answered the call - Mr. Parson, Mr. Gibson and Mr. Sawyer.

The men worked diligently to repair the fallen lines. Their fingers were numb from the cold, but they knew that people depended upon the electricity flowing through these lines. They needed the light and the heat for their homes and to be able cook their food.

The men were carefully replacing the wires when, suddenly and accidentally, the electricity surged back to life in the lines. The terrible jolt of current instantly killed both Mr. Parson and Mr. Gibson. Mr. Sawyer, though badly burned, somehow survived.

He spent many months recovering in the hospital. It was slow and painful. After he had healed, he returned to work at the powerhouse, running it for two or three days a week, doing his best to put the sorrow of the loss of his two friends and coworkers behind him. However, he never did.

The last days of the powerhouse were sad ones. When the men tried to raise the gates for the last time, they became stuck. It was as if the aging building was reluctant to become a piece of history. It was not ready to retire. The march of time, however, is relentless. The men pounded and pounded on the gates until they were finally freed and raised for the last time.

When the powerhouse turbines had been silenced and the impounded waters of Lake Decatur were drained down, the piles of dirt and tree stumps which had been left behind during construction became visible once again.

With the water as low as possible the dam wall was dynamited. As the dust cleared, all that was left was a ridge of dirt and a tangle of rocks and wood. This solid dam which had survived several heavy floods and around fifty years of service was all but obliterated.

However, the old powerhouse is still providing one of the best places to fish in the area. A current still courses through the square opening where the concrete apron was located. Catfish and crappie love it there.

It is said that if you set there very quiet, you can still hear the hum of the turbines echoing over the water of Lake Decatur.

The Game Changer - The Jim Woodruff Dam

In our corner of southwest Georgia, the study for the need of a dam began in the early 1940s. The Rivers and Harbors Act of 1945, became the answer. It authorized a 9 foot deep by 100 foot wide channel to be dug out on the Apalachicola River up the Chattahoochee River to Columbus, Georgia, and also up a segment of the Flint River to Bainbridge. It also laid out a series of dams and the evacuation of the land to be flooded. The actual go ahead to build was authorized in 1945.

The construction started in the early 1950s, with completion in February of 1957.

The location chosen for this dam was where the Flint and Chattahoochee Rivers met with Spring Creek to form the Apalachicola River. Nestled between two high bluffs, this area was a perfect choice for this type of construction and the easiest place to control the flow of the water.

It was discovered that Hernando DeSoto had once camped on these high banks in 1539. DeSoto, who later discovered the Mississippi River, was believed to have been the first white man to see the 80 foot deep gorge carved out by the Chattahoochee and Flint Rivers. These bluffs were naturally formed by silt deposits from these two watery giants.

If you have wondered what the area looked like before the dam, the channel markers that go through the lake, follow the original rivers' routes with the straight lines of the Chattahoochee and the meandering of the Flint coming together in a V just before the dam.

Most of the land which became flooded was already a pond or a swamp. Local residents say most of this area was so thick with vegetation and snakes it was impossible to penetrate. Some stumps of trees are still visible or submerged in shallow waters.

Also, there are the burial mounds in the north end of the lake area which are marked by special pilings. These mounds were thoroughly excavated before the water was restricted. They are now flooded and are marked.

The need for a dam became apparent when the call for more electricity emerged after World War II. Small dams and powerhouses sprang up rather at random, without any system governing their use. For everything to work efficiently, a plan was needed. The answer was a series of dams constructed at special points along the Chattahoochee River and the Flint

River. These dams would not only provide hydroelectric power but also safe navigation along with other related benefits.

It was decided that the Jim Woodruff Dam would be a gravity dam. This is the type that is built of solid concrete and depends primarily on its own weight for stability. Concrete, 15 feet thick at its foundation gradually becomes 3 feet thick at the top. No other structure has more permanence or requires less maintenance than this style dam.

The water levels on each side of the dam are very important to the structure and were determined by studies made by engineers when it was planned. They based these depths on the force exerted on the dam which is called head rating. The water on the low side needs to be maintained as close to 33 feet as possible. The lake's ideal depth is 76 feet.

The dam consists of a fixed spillway, a lock and gated spillway, along with a powerhouse and earthen dike. The spillway is 766 feet long and has 16 vertical lift gates. These release water off the dam. The water impounded turns the turbines which in turn generate electricity.

Too much water flowing through the turbines does not generate more electricity. Quite the opposite. If too much water is falling over the fins which turn the turbines, it actually slows them down. This in turn, slows down the turbines.

Optimum water levels throughout the whole system are maintained as close as possible by a computer system in Mobile, Alabama. It starts upstream at the origin of the Chattahoochee River watershed in Tennessee. The computers try to maintain the ideal water levels for all dams along the system, adjusting for high and low water seasons as well as navigation windows. Some dams in the system have water storage capabilities. The Woodruff Dam has none.

Before computers, as recent as 20 years ago, operators had to deal with the water level on their own. Most operators talked to the weather bureaus. They also kept in touch with each other by radio and telephone. Very little information was available at the time events were happening. This is when the experience of the operators made a difference. They would have to physically look at the water levels and make the decision to raise or lower gates.

The Woodruff Dam is also a part of a very complex electrical generation system. There are several other dams on the Chattahoochee which too are maintained by the Army Corps. of Engineers. However, there are others on the river which are owned by power companies. Most of these are on the Flint River. All of the power which is generated by the dam is distributed as needed by an electrical company in Florida.

Since AC current can't be stored there are two different types of generators in dams. Some run all of the time and some when they are needed called peak generators. This is the type the Woodruff Dam has.

Inside the dam is the powerhouse. It consists of three generation unit bays and an extraction bay. The generator units are 65 feet wide along the centerline. The overall length of the powerhouse is 258 feet by 8 1/2 feet at the foundation.

The dam's control room is a maze of flashing lights, digital readouts, amber lights bubbling out from stark gunmetal gray panels. Knobs and levers join in with toggle switches in a computerized, colorful maze. From this room the turbines are monitored.

Going down 10 feet under the water of Lake Seminole is where the turbine pits and pumping equipment are located. To get to the pit, you go down a dark, narrow hallway. Here you can hear the terrific force of the water slamming against the huge propellers of the turbines.

The inspection gallery is next. It is 31 feet below the water. Here the turbines are accessible through several white metal access doors, the only thing that protects workers from being sucked out into the surging current.

The lowest level is 67 feet down. This is a tunnel that extends through the gated spillway to the lock. This lock provides a 33 foot lift when the lake is at normal pool. The lock walls are 82 feet high and provides for a 5 foot freeboard. The dimensions of the lock are 82 feet wide by 450 feet long. The lock filling and emptying system consists of intake ports built into the upper wall connected by 10 foot by 10 foot chambers. Filling and emptying operations are controlled by automatic valves.

The impact of the dam on southwest Georgia has been enormous. Even though the main purpose of the dam is to provide electricity, aid in navigation and flood control, the fact remains it has provided a fantastic area for lovers of water sports.

Wildlife flocks to Lake Seminole to make it their home. Some species would be extinct if it weren't for this southwest Georgia lake. Recently, the bald eagle population has been increasing in numbers as well as the osprey. The rivers, streams, sloughs and small lakes have long been a haven to a variety of aquatic life. There are also many other reptiles and birds that populate the lake area.

Here are some interesting facts about Lake Seminole. It was named for the Native American, Seminole Indians, who were pushed into Central Florida by the U. S. Army under the direction of Andrew Jackson.

The lake borders both Georgia and Florida as well as Alabama. It has 37,500 acres of water and more than 18,000 acres of surrounding land. It extends up the Chattahoochee River 30 miles and up the Flint River for 35 miles, giving Lake Seminole 376 miles of shoreline.

The dam backed up the waters of the Chattahoochee and Flint Rivers and Spring Creek. Below these bodies of water the dam gave definition to the head of the Apalachicola River.

The sandy soil in the vicinity provides ideal conditions for distinctive coastal plain vegetation like oaks, gums and cypresses. The Lake Seminole region is also dominated by the long needled pines and other conifers and evergreens.

A Surprise Addition - Seminole State Park

There is some very old history represented in Seminole State Park. Records show that in 1675, Franciscan friars tried to start a Spanish mission where the park is today. At the same time, the British were trying to take over the area. After being constantly harassed by the Indians, both the British and the Spanish moved back up the Chattahoochee River and the mission disappeared.

Some evidence of the park's past can be seen in its expansive meadow. As you walk through it, you can't help but notice the tall pines. Imprinted in the bark of some of these stately trees are "cat face" scars, indicating that they were once a part of southwest Georgia's economic past, the turpentine era when the sap from these trees supported the families here. During the Great Depression, the pines kept the residences alive by giving their life blood to bring the necessary economic growth.

As you look at the calm, shimmering water in the lagoon, you may recall that the majority of the land which comprises the park once belong to Crawford Alday. Even today, Alday descendants remember running, playing and riding horses amongst the pines and tangles of vines down to what is now a large lagoon. At one time, this body of water was a shallow pond that made only a slight dip in the terrain. You will also notice the area where there are buoys keeping boaters away. There used to be an island there, complete with trees. They have since rotted and fallen away, but their stumps remain under the water.

Then Georgia Governor, Marvin Griffin, designated the land to be purchased from private owners that was to be used for a state park. The Army Corps. of Engineers was then placed in charge of digging a canal which would connect the existing pond to Fish Pond Drain. These waters would flow inside this lower spot and intensify the bowl shape of the land. The pond would grow into a small lake.

Mr. Cotton Johnson was the first park superintendent, being hired to develop the park in 1960. He planned it in accordance to what he felt would be the best layout. For him, that park was the realization of a dream. Cotton Johnson stayed on as superintendent into the 1990s, when his health no longer allowed him to continue the job. Other original staff members were Roy Barber, Vernon Johnson and Marvin Harrell.

Clearing the park was hard work that went on day and night. Cotton Johnson and Roy Barber were the two men who were the main force that sliced through the wilderness, fighting heat and snakes. However, when the saw dust cleared, they had created a park, complete with roads, picnic shelters, a camp ground and a sandy beach all out of a 343 acre tract of land which was originally covered with trees and underbrush. The then called Marvin Griffin State Park, opened on March 17th, 1960. However, because of political differences, the name was changed to Seminole State Park when the next governor took office.

With a small office and a tiny concession stand built, Cotton turned his energy to creating a camping area. The first part of it was located on the side of the park where the miniature golf is now. At that time, the current camping area was still a tangle of thorny vines and pines, a mere twinkle in Cotton's eye. However, when both camping areas were completed, there were 100 camp sites.

The superintendent's house was built next, then the staff quarters and 10 cabins. This clearing and building took place over a 10 year period. Five of the original cottages were built between 1965 and 1969. Later, five more cottages were added and in 1999, four more were built. Most recently, a heated and air conditioned meeting room, complete with a chef's kitchen has been added for gatherings of up to 200 people.

In the beginning, the most popular area of the park was the beach. At one time, it rivaled Panama City. There were life guards, a diving board, ski shows and a concession stand where food was cooked.

Tickets for the beach were 25 cents. A record was set on one very hot Sunday afternoon when more than 1000 tickets were sold.

In modern day Seminole State Park, there are 50 sites for RV campers, complete with electricity and water hook ups. There is a special spot for pioneer camping. Two comfort stations with hot showers are also in this area.

The rolling green lawns are a picnicker's paradise. Stoves, and 54 tables as well as five shelter houses, provide the perfect setting for fried chicken and potato salad.

If you like to hike there is the 2.2 mile Gopher Tortoise Trail. Walking along this path, through the wildflowers you may get a glimpse of this almost extinct species. Seminole State Park provides a safe area in Georgia where they are still in existence.

Everyone loves their park and frequented it often. Many local people work at the park and most stayed for a long time because they love being a part of it.

Seminole State Park is still a place of beauty with is black pines tickling the delicate blue of the sky and the green, rolling hills. It is also a place of fun, learning, relaxation, communication and sports, a very versatile acreage.

GETTING TO KNOW THE FLINT RIVER

The upper Flint River, just past Bainbridge, will dazzle you. The water is a mesmerizing rainbow of greens and blues. Here the banks are dominated by the ups and downs of the water, steep and more pronounced. There is a hodgepodge of foliage, sand, and rocks worn into unusual shapes by "Mistress River". The evidence shows that on occasion it has had several tantrums because there are places where the trees are barely hanging on to the soil.

Also, here, the river is a world full of sandbars and rocks. Some are hidden from unsuspecting hulls and motor out drives. Others are sticking up, protruding for the sun to warm and the foliage to grow on.

Oddly, up river, the Flint is busy. Unlike the Chattahoochee River, which the farther up you go the more like a primeval jungle it becomes. Way up the Flint, boats and jet skis are everywhere. Homes have become plentiful. Some cling tenuously to the steep and eroded banks. Others are placed far back from the water because one never really knows when the river will explode with fury. Most have just a stretch of wood for a dock for having a boat house is also a very risky business.

You can tell that the Flint River does not like this confinement. She feels claustrophobic in the close constraints of the high sides. Consequently, she seems to rip and claw as she fights her way down river. This is because her instinct has told her that down farther, she will have the freedom to spread her wings. There will be places where she can skitter and play with islands and tiny streams.

This starts to become true once you are down past the railroad bridge and the Highway 84 bridge that follows after. Now, the Flint changes her personality. She becomes a lady who no longer displays her temper. Here, she is reined in, tamed by man with industry and landings. Then surprise, surprise, she changes again. Now, she is like a lady who is sometimes loose, not quite sure of her course or what image she wants to project.

She is a woman who has changed her mind. She does not want to be tame and docile. She doesn't want to be easily maneuvered or easy to get along with. She wants to challenge you. She turns and twists with secret corners and wild shorelines. Sand replaces foliage and knurled tree trunks come in a little closer to your boat than you want.

Now, she begins to show her yearning to wander. She becomes a gypsy, creating tree filled islands and oxbow shaped lakes. Black stumpy areas impose themselves close to channels whose markers show the original course of the river before the dam tried to tame her waywardness.

Now at the mouth, this river loves showing off her party best. The Flint loves to dance and sway. She meanders in countless directions creating little bayous and lakes along the way. Her islands display their presence with exotic abandon with most being green and serene. However, some are dressed up in flowering vines while others show off a tangle of underbrush.

Trees too, put on a spectacular show. Each one is clearly defined even though they sport varying shades of green. It is hard not to think of the wildlife that call these islands and trees home, for they only add to the exotic ambiance of the scene.

Occasionally, the fragrance of honeysuckle and fresh water engulfs your senses as they mingle in the air. Fishermen scatter here, there, everywhere. They hide in their favorite spots. They bob up and down from behind cattail islands and overgrown inlets. All that gives them away are their colorful umbrellas. Now you know, you have reached Lake Seminole.

A Brief Encounter With The Flint River

When the Spanish explorer, DeSoto, came to claim this area for the Spanish in 1539, he called this river *Capachequii*, which means Flint. However, on another ancient Spanish map which was dated at around the same time, the river was called *Rio Pernales*.

In 1719, the "Atlas Englishman" used the name Flint for the river. Then in 1776, William Bartram tells about crossing the Flint in his chronicles of his explorations here. A later French map done in 1781, calls the Flint, *River Au Callaux*. The Creek and Cherokee Indians called it *Thronateeska,* the Indian word for Flint. As early as the 1800s, white settlers also called her *Thronateeska*. Eventually, after the Indians had left the river area, the name became Flint and it stayed once and for all.

By any name, it is a cool refreshing river which flows down from near Atlanta to the Woodruff Dam. As a thin line, it meanders its way through several towns one being Andersonville, sight of the Civil War prison. Then, getting wider, more powerful, it goes on through Albany and on to Bainbridge. From there it goes down until it stops at the dam, where it mingles with the Chattahoochee River and Spring Creek to feed the Apalachicola River.

The Flint River has seen a great variation in water traffic. Explorers have paddled down through her waters, and past her woodlands. Such names like Ponce de Leon, DeSoto and Andrew Jackson and many Indian tribes camped on her banks.

The Flint River has been the site of several historic forts. In 1665, the British troops set up a campsite on the western ridge of the Flint. A fever spread by mosquitoes took a toll and this fort was abandoned. It is seen on early maps as the British burial ground.

In the early 1800s, the U. S. Army built Fort Scott almost across from present day Wingate's Lunker Lodge. It was small and provided temporary safety from the Indians for the settlers. However, the same species of mosquitoes which infected the British also infected the Army. Those stricken were taken to Camp Recovery, which was on high ground across and away from the river.

Several Indian battles were fought on and around the Flint River before peace came to this area. Once here, steamboat traffic became plentiful. There were many ferry landings along the Flint.

Today, there still are many landings, most of which are under the jurisdiction of the Army Corps. of Engineers. Picnic tables now set where Indian battles took place and prehistoric pottery and bones were found. Let's become better acquainted with the history of this fantastically beautiful river and its landings. There are a quite a few places that provide interesting stories about the river and her area. Here are some.

History On The Edge - The Apalachicola Fort

On a map, made a long, long time ago, there is a notation, written in fading black ink on a very yellow parchment-like piece of paper. It notes that on the west side of Spring Creek, near where it joins the Flint River and the Chattahoochee River, there existed a village called the Apalachicola Fort.

Its description places it right in the area where the Flint and Chattahoochee Rivers met, known as the Forks. However, it is believed that at one time there were 12 sites in the Forks that followed a line from the mouth of the Flint to Hare's Landing, which is now the Wildlife Management Area Landing, on the Chattahoochee River. Of these 12, only two are believed to have been permanent settlements. The others were just stop overs for hunting and fishing parties of Indians. The Apalachicola Fort is believed to have been one of these permanent settlements. This encampment probably was more like a fort than a village. When it was built, a four foot high earthen mound was constructed around it for defense.

Some early maps place the Apalachicola Fort closer to the mouth of Spring Creek. However, excavations done before the Woodruff Dam was built, revealed artifacts that place the fort in the Forks more towards the Flint River side. It is here that archeologists found evidence that ancient and on up to more modern Indians and also white men lived and fought in this area throughout the ages.

The first Indians of record to reside in the Forks were the Apalachee. They were located along the Apalachicola River and over most of southwest Georgia. According to Creek legends, the Apalachee lived here when the Muskogee Indians invaded the area around 1639. The Apalachee were almost completely wiped out.

Some evidence of life was located by Joseph Caldwell from the Smithsonian Institute. He found pottery of a late design, iron and copper nails, two large and one small flint guns and part of a house with European artifacts in a trench. It is likely that this was the sight of the fort.

Evidence was found along a four mile stretch between the Flint River and Spring Creek that tells of a village that consisted of 24 houses placed in a square where 13 families lived. The settlement was defended by 22 gunmen.

In 1679, a Spanish Friar, Juan Oacon and two others were sent to Sabacola, a village on the Chattahoochee River near modern day Columbus, Georgia. They were to come down the river and establish a mission. Once done, they were to help others go down the Chattahoochee to build more missions.

In March of 1681, these two Franciscan friars, Pedro Gutierrez and Miguel Abenzaja, marched from the above mentioned Sabacola down to the Forks area. There they set up Santa Cruz de Sabacola at the confluence of the rivers not far from what was believed to be an earlier Franciscan Mission built in 1660 that had been abandoned. Santa Cruz was built on the east bank. However, the Indians were not consulted before it was established and again they chased the friars away.

In 1685, Antonio Matheos, with a force of Spaniards and mission Indians, went down to the Forks to rebuild. He tried five times to stay there but was chased away by the local tribes every time.

Finally, in 1689, the friars from the Sabacola mission by Columbus, once again moved down river to the Forks. Again, they established the Mission of Santa Cruz de Sabacola and also another new mission called Chatots de Sabacola located just a little ways from the mouth on the west side of the Forks by the Flint River.

A new century dawned and the Forks was also the sight of a battle in 1702. This was a fight between the English and Spanish. The English wanted to settle this area and sent fur traders to colonize it. However there was a constant battle between the Spanish and the English as both desired control. The Spanish especially desired the valuable rivers. There were uprisings everywhere. The difference came when the Spanish were able to make friends with the Indians and the English couldn't seem to do this.

The first recorded Indians to live where the Apalachicola Fort existed are believed to have been what was left of the Muskogee tribe after its war with the Lower Creeks in 1686. Sometime around 1750, the Creek Indians abandoned the fort and went higher up the Chattahoochee River.

In 1769, the Spanish army came and took over the missions and joined everything together, reviving and enlarging the Apalachicola Fort. However, after about 15 years, it was abandoned again.

When archeologists excavated the Forks, they found a bayonet from an English Army gun bearing the marks of the 46th Infantry Regiment of the English Army. According to historical notes, this regiment was here in 1776, on its way to Florida and then on to the West Indies.

We do know for sure that there was a settlement between the Chattahoochee and Flint Rivers, and more than likely, it was the Apalachicola Fort. However, by the 1800s, the exact location was lost.

Throughout history maps mention the fort. Henry Popple, who drew a map in 1733, called the fort in the area Palachucola. It designates the Chattahoochee River and an unnamed river most likely the Flint.

A map in the Library of Congress shows a survey done in 1763. The legend of this map shows a four pointed star with an enclosure around it. This designates the existence of a settlement on the banks of the Flint River, just below the mouth of Spring Creek.

A map from around 1829, mentions the Apalachicola Fort and describes the area as an extensive fortification with a bank two or three feet higher at the junction of the Chattahoochee and Flint Rivers.

Once again the Spaniards tried to start a settlement there, but they abandoned this idea in favor of the St. Marks area because it was easier to approach.

We will never know for sure where the fort existed. However, we do know that the Indians, both ancient and modern, as well as many white men found our area to be just like we feel -beautiful.

Not As Cuddly As Its Name - The Battle Of The Blankets

One of the very first battles to be documented on the Flint River was given the name, Battle Of The Blankets. This occurred in 1702. It was a chance encounter by two large, well armed groups of men who met in what was then a pine forest. The result was a massacre.

Although little is known about it, this battle is considered to be the first blood of a war known as the Queen Anne War. It was about the fight to dominate in America and it raged between the English and the Spanish.

Even though this battle took place here, thousands of miles from Europe, it had a profound affect upon the English and Spanish. At this time, the Spanish were trying to take over the three rivers for Spain by enlisting the help of the Apalachee Indians. The English wanted this land for themselves and had the Creeks for allies.

The battle seems to have come about through a twist of fate. To start with, a Creek force of 400 warriors departed from a meeting in the town of Hitchiti and headed toward the Apalachee missions in the area between the Flint River and the Chattahoochee River. This party included Creek men and one woman, Chisca men and 10 Westo men with three Westo women. They were very well armed with guns, a large amount of gun powder and knives. They joined with the English. The leader of this coalition was Lieutenant Anthony. The date of their departure is not clear, but it was probably around October 6, 1702.

The other players in this battle were the Spanish and Apalachee Indians, as well as warriors from the Chacato and Timucua tribes. The Spanish leader was Francisco Romo de Uriza. They were seeking revenge on the Creeks for a recent attack on a mission, Santa Fe de Teleco, and also the murder of one of their leaders.

The Indians numbered around 800 and the Spanish force was only around 30 soldiers. They were all armed with bows and arrows and war clubs, which left them at a significant disadvantage even though they outnumbered the Creek and English force.

The Spanish and the Apalachee Indian forces marched north along a trail that would eventually take them to the lower Flint River. The English and the Creek Indians force marched south along this same trail.

On an evening in late October, these forces met on the banks of the Flint River near where Bainbridge is today. Both English and Creeks were aware that the Spanish and their allies were moving close to their encampment and decided to set a trap. Knowing the Spanish liked to attack at dawn, the English stuffed their blankets with straw, set the camp fires burning low and then hid in the woods. When the Spanish attack came, the English sprang from hiding and slaughtered some 600 of the Spanish forces. The rest were captured and sold as slaves to the plantations in the Carolinas.

The women who came along with the Spanish were believed to have ran into the Georgia forest where they hid, shielded by the pines. One account given by a Chacato Indian woman tells about how she came upon the English camp. She knew this because there was evidence left behind that they had stopped there and spent the night. She figured that the English were taking many prisoners because she found many wooden locks they had left behind that were used to secure the prisoners for the night. She also saw the many dead at the battle site itself.

When going by her account of time and direction, it seems that the battle took place on Thursday, October 12, 1702.

It also figures that the battle site was somewhere on the Flint River where Bainbridge exists now. However, it is most likely the actual place of the battle will never be known because of the lack of evidence and what was there is now destroyed.

Although details were scarce and often there are conflicting stories, we do know that there was this major battle in which many Indians lost their lives.

First Named By Roving Indians And A Trader Man - Bainbridge

The land along the Flint River is very, very old. So many footsteps! Some large-belonging to warriors. Some tiny, those of a child's first hesitant step. Others may be from the old, whose feet knew the pain of being crippled.

In places, blood has stained this earth. Some from an arrow of war, still others are drops from a new birth. Through all of the thousands of years of the past, one single thing has been true and that is the Flint River. It may be angry, flowing swiftly, overflowing its banks as it is gorged with rain water, or low and slow during a drought, as it just begs for a drop or two of precious rain.

However, on a parcel of land known as Lot 223, in Grimsley Field, along the Flint River, many people joined together and formed settlements.

All this probably began 8000 maybe 10,000 years ago. Roaming ancient Indians found life on the banks of the Flint was much to their liking. There was great fishing, abundant wildlife for hunting and the famous red mud for making pots and other utensils.

The first documented of these villages was a Creek Indian settlement known as Pucknawhitla. It rested on the river's high banks, some 75 feet above the water on the east side of the Flint, somewhere near where Chason Park is now.

This village is said to have existed in 1765. How long it was there, no one knows. However, on a map drawn in 1745, by the Spanish, it is thought to have been in existence. The map has many symbols on it and some look like cabins, the same style that the Creek Indians built.

Most Indian towns were temporary settlements and that makes them difficult to locate with accuracy. The Indians would leave when the hunting and fishing would no longer be abundant or because of the smell of rotting bones from garbage and the human waste became overwhelming. They would pack up and go elsewhere to set up a new settlement. It is believed that some of the Indians at Pucknawhitla left and settled on the lower Chattahoochee River while others stayed on.

Also, somewhere in this area, it is believed that the first trading post on the Flint existed. It was called Burgess on some very old maps and Burgess Town on some others. Historians may not totally agree on the name of the town. However, they do concur that the plot of land named District 15 on an original map of Early County dated in the very early 1800s, and then divided down to be called land Lot No. 224, was once the site of the trading post, next to Pucknawhitla. Now, these lands are part of the growing port city of Bainbridge.

Burgess was built by and named after its founder, James Burgess. His name is mentioned in our area as early as 1765. James was described in the diary of Rebecca Sherwood, who eventually became the co-owner of the Panton-Leslie Trading Company, as a white man who married several Indian women of the Lower Creek tribe. He came from Florida and was also an express rider. His name is mentioned as a fur trader who came to the Creek Indian town of Tamatley, which was located on the western bank of the Apalachicola River.

When studying a map from 1778, Burgess the town is shown on the Flint. However, there is another town called Burgess in Alabama. It wasn't until on a map from 1820, that a clearer picture of Burgess appeared. This map has symbols that are believed to be the sites of cabins, which made up Burgess. However, it is believed that Burgess was abandoned at this time.

Now, all of the signs that a town existed are gone. Even though white man lived here for more than 250 years, nothing remains but these symbols on a map. No artifacts were ever found or archeological digs ever done in this area.

Further evidence that Burgess existed near where Fort Hughes later was built was mentioned in some letters that soldiers who were passing through wrote. They said that James Burgess had a store near Pucknawhitla, an Indian town 30 miles above the Forks. This places it where Bainbridge is today.

Therefore, we can be sure that James Burgess had a store. It is also likely that he got his trade goods on credit from the Panton-Leslie Company, thus coming in contact with Rebecca Sherwood.

It is also believed that he had several stores in and around the Flint River, Pucknawhitla and Burgess area, or, he could have had a rolling store and that he visited several areas. James seemed to be an enterprising man who maintained a high stock of trade goods.

Legends about Burgess state that he had three Creek Indian wives. For there to be peace and harmony in his household, he would have had to live in three different places, because unless the wives were sisters, all would have been chaos. This theory has more merit because this would have placed him in several areas where it was believed that he had trading posts.

Also, his wives would have helped in the stores especially when he was gone.

Burgess was also very active in the 1790s, when the Spanish influence in our area was strong. He usually appeared to be on the side of the Spanish. However, if it was more advantageous for him to be on the American side, he could switch over in a heartbeat.

It was around this time when he came in contact with Augustus Bowles, a famous pirate on our rivers. It was during this association that Burgess was accused of stealing goods from his rival trader, James Seagrove. During this robbery two men were killed.

At this time the Indian agent was John Kinnard. He ordered Burgess to appear before him and surrender the stolen goods. However, Burgess said he was innocent and it was three Indians who were paid by the Panton-Leslie Company to do this to their business rival. He also said that the murders were committed by Indians from Pensacola.

From some business ledgers of the Panton-Leslie Company, we find that in 1797, Burgess visited St. Marks in Florida, where he bought trade goods from their warehouse.

It is believed Burgess died around 1800, because he is not mentioned after that date. However, the town seemed to have outlived him. In a survey done in 1820, it was recorded that the town of Burgess was once about one mile up river from Fort Hughes. This would place it just past the railroad bridge and the Elberta Crate Company dock. It may have been close to the site of what is now Oak City Cemetery.

Later records indicate that the town was abandoned in 1818. This is around the same time that Fort Hughes was dismantled. If someone had explored here, who knows what history they would have found.

Touching a Ghostly Hand - Fort Hughes

High up on a bluff, overlooking the Flint River is the site of the first defensive fort in our area for protection against the attacks of the Seminole Indians, Fort Hughes. It was not an imposing bastion, rather just a small block building and a surrounding stockade on two acres of land.

During the time that the Spanish occupied Florida, they came to our area. By following the road known as El Camino Real, meaning the King's Highway, it led them to the waters of the Flint River on March 5, 1540. They called their find *River de Capcheque*. Here, where Fort Hughes would stand some 250 years in the future, they constructed a barge and crossed over.

In 1778, their route was found on a map drawn by Joseph Purcell. It connected St. Augustine and Pensacola, then followed on up to the Flint. It was little more than a pathway used by traders who set up posts for the Panton-Leslie Trading Company, a large business at that time.

Many Indians occupied the high cliffs along the Flint where now Bainbridge is located. This was their home long before white man arrived. It is known that the Indians lived here in 1765, and that their settlement was known as Pucknawhitla. Later in time, this settlement was taken over by John Burgess who established a trading post. This area became known as Burgess.

When Fort Hughes was built in 1817, the area was renamed after the fort and was known by that name until 1823, when Decatur County was created.

Established by the 4th and 7th Infantry, Fort Hughes was occupied by the Army for only several months in the fall of 1817. However, no matter how humble, it was an important outpost at the time because it protected one of the main crossings on the Flint River.

During the battle with the Seminole Indians at Fowlstown, bugler Aaron Hughes, a very young soldier, stood upon an Indian cabin and was shot and killed by an Indian who was under cover. This was on November 28, 1817. Two men were wounded there. However, Hughes was the only casualty of this encounter.

When Fort Hughes was built, it was decided to name this fort after young bugler, Hughes. The camp was to be protection for town's people from the marauding Indians, who attacked the settlement at Fowlstown. It also served as an arsenal during the first of several wars with the Seminole Indians.

In 1817, Lt. Col. Arbuckle, commanding officer at Fort Scott, assigned Captain John M. McIntosh to be commander at Fort Hughes.

On December 15, 1817, Arbuckle wrote General Gaines that a post 12 miles north of Fort Scott, under the command of McIntosh, along with 50 men, had been surrounded for several days by 200 to 300 Indians, but the attackers had been beaten off with no fatalities.

On December 20, 1817, Captain McIntosh wrote of the difficulty of supplying Fort Hughes during this past battle. He recounted what it was like getting supplies up 12 miles during the fighting.

Since Fort Hughes was dependent upon Fort Scott for supplies, their situation became critical because the Indians could easily stop them.

In 1824, Fort Hughes became a ferry service landing that was started by William Moody. He was a soldier under Andrew Jackson. When he marched through here early in the 1800s, he liked the area and eventually settled here. He kept his ferry running for several years.

Now the fort area is the site of J. D. Chason Memorial Park which was dedicated by the Chason family in memory of the late Dr. Chason on December 29, 1921. They also wanted to preserve this historic place.

In the park, the fort site and Hughes's grave are marked with a cannon. Originally, a cannon was also placed at Fort Scott and one at Camp Recovery. These three cannons were brought here by Congressman Henry G. Turner, who persuaded Secretary of War, Robert L. Lincoln, to give them to Decatur County. They came from Fort Clinch, in Fernandina, Florida. The 7,200 pound cannon was brought to Bainbridge in 1882. It was capable of firing a 32 pound shell. The *Bainbridge Democrat* of May 24, 1883, states, "Fort Hughes's monument is mounted." It was presumed that the others were erected at the same time.

Now there are two cannons in the park. The cannon that was originally at the site of Fort Scott was moved to Chason Park in the late 1950s when the Woodruff Dam backed up the waters of the rivers and Fort Scott became a victim of the flood. The cannon at Camp Recovery is still there.

Captain McIntosh gave this honor to the men: United States soldiers at Fort Hughes, Fort Scott and Camp Recovery found and took possession of these lands for the United States."

Skeletons Still Rise - Fort Scott

The water that goes by Fort Scott is beautiful in a rare and sensuous way that invites the past to grab you anytime and anywhere. Mist is predominant, hiding the fine line between earth and sky, between fantasy and reality.

As you navigate through the Fort Scott Islands, you are greeted by the pungent odor of the past. Huge trees darken the sun's light and ghostly faces greet you in the thick underbrush. Egrets scream and marsh hens cackle a warning to their kind upstream. They sense that an intruder is entering the sacred waters which along with any number of ghosts, they call home. It does not matter, we are determined to go forward into this haven of the unknown.

A blast of cold air causes chills to run up the spine, causing shivers.

Why is this area so very cold and forbidding while elsewhere in the channel it is warm and inviting? Is it because amongst this wild tangle of vines and snakes there once was the fortification known as Fort Scott, where so many had died?

The loneliness here takes your breath away! It hangs like the dew on a hot, sticky morning. Vegetation and trees encroach the water way. Mats of dying weeds brush your boat. Your imagination wants you to try and picture what life was like, way back then, in the early 1800s. It wants you to see that this very passage may have been but a trickle, which turned into a broad creek after a heavy rain.

It begs you to try to remember that the height of the banks through the cutoff was once considered high bluffs and that this land was far above the level of the modern day waters of the Flint River.

Built in 1816, Fort Scott was never meant to be a permanent structure. It was to be a temporary defense against the Seminole Indians and for a while it provided a haven for approximately 300 soldiers. It didn't even start out being called Fort Scott but Camp Crawford. However, in February of 1817, it was called Fort Scott in a letter that was written from one soldier to another.

Construction of the fort was on the west bank of the Flint River, a few miles above where its waters mixed into those of the Chattahoochee. Also adjacent to Fort Scott, were several large springs, a part of Spring Creek. At this time, behind the fort, the crystal clear, very inviting waters of Spring Creek bubbled up. It was noted in several letters that at this time, the creek was 8 to 10 inches deep and 10 to 12 feet wide.

Built by the Army's Fourth Regiment, Fort Scott was made of logs. The barracks were small and constructed of squared logs. The floors were earthen. The buildings were planned close together, all in one line, parallel to the Flint River and about 100 yards inland. The officer's quarters were built in the middle of the line of barracks.

As far as its armament, there were only two - 24-pound guns. It was believed that this would be sufficient because the barracks were built so that by closing the doors and windows, they were secure in the front. Then by closing the picket work, the back was secure.

Fort Scott was a very important frontier post. When it first opened, the settlers started to migrate to it for safety. There were hostile Indians all around it, and it was only about six miles from Spanish territory. You can see where these three neighbors did not get along since they all wanted the same parcel of land. Also, there were reports of massacres around Fowlstown. This caused Fort Scott to become a home for refugees making it a very busy place.

However, its location was the fort's downfall. First of all, the Indians could easily stop supplies from getting there. In the best of times, it was difficult. During battle, it was practically impossible and many people died of starvation.

First, the cargo had to come from New Orleans, Louisiana, and Mobile, Alabama, on through the Gulf of Mexico. Then the boatmen had to work to navigate their way up the shallow, cypress stump riddled Apalachicola River. If the breezes blew hard enough, the boats were sailed up river. When breezes stopped, however, the men had to use poles to push upstream against the current.

Supplies also came to the fort by an over-land route. However, this too included the hazards of the marauding Indians. You can see where getting supplies was always a problem.

During the Seminole Indian Wars, Fort Scott was under siege for long periods of time. The Indians didn't take it over, but by blocking supplies, they brought the troops to near starvation.

Secondly, the Fort was surrounded by swamps and dampness. Diseases easily flourished and one third of the men there died from yellow fever and dysentery.

Perhaps the best way to picture the few years of U. S. Army life at Fort Scott is to go through some letters now on file in the Library of Congress in Washington D. C. written by the men who were stationed there. Most men tell of many nuisance strikes by the Indians who forced settlers from their homes by raids, taking their cattle and sometimes their lives.

One of the most famous battles which took place near Fort Scott was in November, 1817. A large party of soldiers and passengers were ambushed on the Apalachicola River at a place where the banks of the river were high and the passage narrow. This was where the Woodruff Dam now exits.

On a small, shallow draft keel boat, about 40 soldiers, most of whom were sick, accompanied seven wives of soldiers, who were dressed as military men. This small party was making its way down the Flint River. However, the current in the area was quite strong and the boat had to be kept near the shoreline.

Unseen by those on the boat, the Indians formed a line along the shore. Suddenly, they attacked. The soldiers on board returned fire. However, the conditions on the boat were so crowded that they could barely maneuver around each other. Nevertheless, when the melee ceased only six men, four of whom were wounded and one woman escaped.

This attack on the boat was believed to have happened early in the day. Help from Fort Scott didn't arrive till nightfall. By this time the shooting was over. However, this was the beginning of a siege on the fort that lasted about four weeks. During this time, supplies were running out at the fort creating a desperate situation. Guns and ammo, as well as food, were almost gone and the enemy was still firmly holding both sides of the Flint River. It was estimated that between 800 to 1200 Indians had gathered with more coming every day.

The best account of this attack is in a letter written by Major Muhlenberg, who told how the soldiers valiantly fought back. He told of how they were pinned down by the guns of the Indians. He also states how over half of these soldiers at the fort were sick with malaria or dysentery. After many agonizing days, the Indians left Fort Scott to the U.S. Army.

After 1821, the Army left Fort Scott and it became a civilian settlement. At this time there were 396 soldiers, 82 of whom were sick and 22 had died in the four month period just prior to the closing.

It has been surmised that John Griffin created a ferry crossing across the Flint at Fort Scott. This is because of a bill presented to the Georgia State Legislature in 1821.

The fort continued to be occupied by civilians until sometime in 1848. A small city was started there by a couple of settlers. A trading post is said to have existed until about 1882, because of a mention in the newspaper which stated it was a major trading center.

Now the site of Fort Scott lies mainly beneath the waters of Lake Seminole. However, long before the waters of the lake covered the land, the physical evidence of the fort was gone. All that remains are the ghosts and several islands which comprise this cutoff connecting the Flint River to Spring Creek.

History Long Buried - Camp Recovery

In a lonely, grassy field about 200 feet from the pavement of Booster Club Road in Decatur County, is one of the oldest historic sites along the Flint River that still exists, Camp

Recovery. Here the U. S. Army tried to establish a field hospital for the men of Fort Scott.

The need for Camp Recovery came from the fact that there were quite a few deaths at nearby Fort Scott, not from fighting Indians, but from a variety of diseases. Consequently, the fort had a bad reputation and soldiers did not want duty there for this reason.

This condition existed simply because Fort Scott was built too close to swamp lands. True it was on higher ground, but the surrounding area was mostly under water. Mosquitoes love this kind of environment and the diseases which they carry, malaria and yellow fever, were as common as a cold.

This type of landscape also promoted unsanitary conditions. Latrines were shallow and filled up fast. They had to be moved often. This promoted dysentery and typhoid, making these diseases also common among the soldiers.

To help cure the many men who mostly battled diseases, Camp Recovery was set up across the Flint in 1820, up on very high bluffs. The evacuation began on September 15th with some 70 severely ill men being transported to the tent hospital which had been erected in a cleared field across the river.

The men had barely gotten themselves settled when a five day rain set in. This onset of cool, wet weather caused deaths amongst the men, claiming the weakest ones first.

After this devastating beginning, life did start to get better. Everyone held out hope for the recovery of the remaining men, but the ideal conditions did not last. Late in October, the temperature fell to an unusual low and once again, men died.

This was another devastating blow to the recovery effort. More men had been lost than saved. Because of this, it was felt that it would be best to close Camp Recovery. On November 23, 1820, the area was evacuated.

All in all, most of the 70 men which were brought over to the camp died and were buried in a clearing several yards from the tent hospital.

Camp Recovery is just a short drive from the confines of the city of Bainbridge, but once visitors are there, they may feel like they are a million miles from civilization.

High above the Flint River, its waters can be seen, glistening below the trees and shrubs of the near-by homes. Cannons were no doubt here when the noise of the camp invaded this quiet spot. Now, there is a kind of loneliness that hangs like a smothering blanket in the air.

The grassy meadow where the camp once existed is a short walk to a block building that marks the entrance to a cool, shady field. Here, more than 195 years ago, the large canvas tent, furnished with wood and cloth cots, was occupied by men in need. Now there is a fairly small block building denoting where the hospital stood. This sturdy building may have within its walls, flowers and mementos, put there by visitors as a memorial for those who were here so very long ago during that fatal fall.

Exiting the building, visitors come upon where the cemetery is marked by a cannon standing in an upright position in the shade of an oak tree so huge that it totally blocks the sun's light. Somewhere below this earth, under more than a century and a half of leaves and dirt, are the long dead soldiers. What were their names? Were they far from home? Were they so very young that they had not yet lived? Were they desperately lonely? Did they find comfort?

The markers which bore their names and regiment were made of pine and have long since decayed. However, the local historical society has maintained the ground and helped sustain the men's memories.

Success For A Hope And A Dream - *The Refuge*

Charles Lewis Munnerlyn had a dream. He was a man of purpose and when he set his mind to do something, he did it. Therefore, seeing that he was the first documented owner of a large tract of land along the Flint River, was not surprising. Originally from South Carolina, Charles Lewis first settled in Florida in 1833. There are no records which say why he felt that the Florida land was not the place where he could pursue his dream of being the owner of a large plantation. Therefore, he gathered his family and his slaves together and traveled to southwest Georgia. Here he found the fertile lands along the banks of the Flint River the ideal place to set up his homestead. This was in 1837. The Munnerlyn group had to have been very brave for at this time the Seminole and Creek Indians were still raiding settler's homes in this area of Georgia.

Charles L. was considered to be a wealthy man. His wife, Hannah White Shackelford Munnerlyn, was the descendant of a large, wealthy family which added to the existing Munnerlyn fortune.

After the original land purchase, Charles L. kept buying parcels of land until in 1860, the plantation was made up of over 3000 acres on the east bank of the Flint River. It is in this area that they built their grand home which was known as *The Refuge*. It has been described in several history books as having "broad verandas, wide halls and airy rooms. All of this was surrounded by well kept lawns, a huge English flower garden and a kitchen garden."

The mansion was also, "in the middle of two vine covered cottages which were used as guest houses where everyone, even strangers, were made welcome".

Several historians think that the Munnerlyn estate was also a place where the Alligator Stage Coach Line stopped. It operated between the 1830s, until after the Civil War in 1865.

History describes Charles L. Munnerlyn as a grand and noble Southern gentleman. He also was a shrewd and successful business man who had a reputation for dealing fairly with everyone including his workers.

His wife, Hannah, gave birth to several children but only one lived to adulthood and that was Charles James Munnerlyn. He was born in 1822, while the family was still living in South Carolina.

The large plantations had their own landings for the steamboats to dock. They would load the ship with their cargo which was mostly cotton. Munnerlyn's Landing was believed to have been at the foot of a now impassible road called Lambert's Ferry. Here the steamboat, *Callahan*, docked several times a week.

The Union blockade and wartime conditions threatened the way of life along the rivers by restricting travel along the waterways. The familiar, privileged life of the Munnerlyns was choked off around 1862.

Charles L. did not live to see the strife of the Civil War nor the tragic burning of *The Refuge* in a devastating fire in 1883. Charles Lewis died in 1857, at the age of 71. Once a strong man, he may have developed Alzheimer's disease for some accounts tell of him becoming quite feeble and dependent upon his wife and Charles J. for him to function in life. It tells us that his mental capacity became impaired.

Workers at modern day Southlands Experimental Forest which is situated on most of the land owned by Charles L., have searched the area for the location of the Munnerlyn mansion. The house was believed to have been about 500 feet from where the Munnerlyn Cemetery sits.

Forest workers have found a place where the planting of certain bushes and trees seem to frame an area where a large structure had once stood. They searched and searched there with metal detectors but nothing definitive was found.

Surrounded by a wrought iron fence, the Munnerlyn Cemetery is the only evidence that the family had left behind as proof that they lived here and made an impact on the area. However, there is an interesting legend that goes along with the cemetery. Seems that in 1934, a huge fire engulfed the fields in Southlands. It burned and burned despite the efforts of many people to stop it. Finally, it burned itself out. Workers went out to investigate how much damage was done. They found that the fire had burned everything up to and around the cemetery, but had stopped at the iron fence. Nothing in the plot had been touched by fire. From this time on, workers did not want to go in this area because they believed that it was haunted.

GETTING TO KNOW THE CHATTAHOOCHEE RIVER

The Chattahoochee River is quite the opposite of the Flint. Unlike its shorter counterpart, this river, except for by its mouth, has a well defined direction. Her swift, deep current carries water down a green, velvet ribbon to Lake Seminole below. She remains steadfast and true in her mission. Her single mindedness dares anyone to penetrate her concentration and discover her secrets.

This river does have its wild places. It writhes and twists and turns with beauty exploding around each bend. Half drowned trees bob and bow as the water rushes by. The sunshine gives warmth and definition to the land that serves as the boundary for the river. The high, sandy banks are filled with channels and gouges. The earth seems to dive down, as if for a drink, then melts right into the waters below.

This river is really an untamed waterway. She can run wild and wicked, an unruly stripe of brown water with a current that has a definite attitude. Even though dams try to tame her down, on occasion, she does break loose. Then, every so often, she goes on a rampage. The evidence of the high, very strong currents caused by the heavy spring rains show up in the fact that many trees are strewn everywhere along the banks, their roots exposed to the hot sun, their branches and leaves left to wither and die.

Down towards the dam, the river's shape is wide, with lazy currents that go around bits of islands that create scraps of side channels. They purposely distract your attention from the main waterway. Here the river's sides are low and swampy. She deposit's the silt which she has collected on her journey here, like so many souvenirs of her travels. So thick are these deposits that they built very high banks on the sides. So rich are these deposits that they supported four villages at four different time periods back in history. However now they are spread throughout Lake Seminole.

A Brief Encounter With The "Hooch"

The Chattahoochee River has always been very popular, from prehistoric times to now. Spaniard, Ponce de Leon, traveled the river down to the Gulf of Mexico, looking for his Fountain of Youth. Missionaries traveled her while trying to find places to build churches and convert the Indians.

This mighty river begins as a small trickle of water near Popular Stump by Horse Trough Mountain in Union County, Georgia. Imagine, a small trickle that anyone can just step across grows to be one of the mightiest rivers in America. It has carried deposits from countless creeks and streams for some two million years.

On its trip down from the mountains it passes by big cities, small cities and pristine towns as well as wild, untamed wetlands. Touching her waters is like grasping on to an ancient life, a link to the past of man in southwest Georgia. A living entity, it continues on to form the boarder between Georgia and Alabama and Georgia and Florida.

Many dreams have unfolded on this river. Bravery, pageantry, cruelty, beauty and tragedy, the banks of the Chattahoochee has seen it all. Some stories are of Indians who stalked their game and lived peaceful lives. Some Indians were warriors who fought when they became disturbed or enraged.

Explorers traveled the river, adventure constantly at their heels. Still others were soldiers and politicians. Some used the water to make a living for themselves and their family on the riverboats. Many have sung songs and wrote poems about this major river.

Its history spans the time from the prehistoric Indians and the Spanish to the Civil War and then on through the steamboat and barge days to the bass boats and jet skis of modern times. There is no telling how much history now is covered by the waters.

The Indians called this 436 mile river the *Chatta-hucha*. *Chatta* is Choctaw for red. *Hucha* is the word for river. The Cherokee called the river *Chatt-cho-chee* or river of painted rocks. Apparently, in the upper reaches of the river, the rocks were stained red and pink by nature. The Indians thought this to be the will of God. The present day spelling has not changed much and the original meaning not at all

There are numerous access ramps and parks on the Chattahoochee.

The entrances to these landings reminds one of the Amazon River with their heavy vegetation. In the past, the river has seen canoes, steamboats, war ships, dredges, tug boats and barges. Now she hosts bass boats and pontoon boats.

Choked By Water - Hare's Landing (Wildlife Management Area)

The waters at Hare's Landing hold many secrets. Some are dark and mysterious while others are crystal and shiny. Some are submerged under clear water while others flourish in the green darkness of the swamp. Even though the utmost effort has been made to explore the land and save its relics, the spirits of these Georgians of the past cannot be gathered up and placed in a glass case. For who knows whose footsteps walked on this land before time was measured. Now, those footsteps have long been washed from the earth. Their wishes drowned by the encroaching waters. However, their spirits do live on.

The first archeological dig at Hare's Landing took place in 1901 and was done by Charles Moore. He found two large burial mounds which were around 10,000 years old. This macabre site was in a swamp on the banks of what once was Curry Lake, about a mile and a half south and east of the where the landing is now. At the time of the discovery, the banks of the Chattahoochee were about 700 feet away.

These very important finds were described as being 5 feet high and 48 feet across with a sandy base. Existing amidst a thickening fog and out of control vegetation, they were fairly intact and undisturbed by humans.

When Moore opened the mound, he reported finding at least 43 burials there, most only two feet below the surface. However, they were so fragmented that they were unrecognizable as human bone until tests confirmed what they were. All the burials were on the west side of the mound.

In several instances bunched burials were found. Also some were found in a form called a flexed burial. One of these showed a distinct skeleton, flexed, lying on its back with a mass of charcoal beside the skull.

In a number of cases charcoal phosphate rock were with the bones. This helped some what as a protection from moisture.

Moore stated that no artifacts were found with any of the burials. However, he did find pottery at the east end in the mound. Cup fragments, hammer stones, mica and stone tools were also there. Moore did not find the pottery interesting and he did not identify most of the markings. He described them as "faint and carelessly impressed".

In 1948, the Army Corps. Of Engineers called on the University of Georgia to come and explore the area for artifacts before the water would cover up all of the history. However, because after Moore left, man came and occupied this land, it had been plowed. The trees and vegetation in the area changed and they failed to find this site. It was not rediscovered until the land was cleared of trees and vegetation in 1954, in final preparation for Lake Seminole. This is when the Smithsonian Institute was called to investigate for this was now a part of a major find which started at Fairchild Landing and came all the way down to where Hare's Landing, now the WMA Landing, exists. Dr. Joseph Caldwell was in charge of this dig.

There were many mounds found in the Hare's Landing area. Some were for shells and animal bones, others held broken pottery. These pottery and shell finds were numerous. One particularly large area was 50 feet long and 25 feet wide, while another was 75 feet long and 35 feet wide. Caldwell categorized all of his finds.

When the pottery found in Moore's burial mound was compared to the pottery found in other areas, they discovered that there was a specific type of design used for mortuary purposes. Also, they concluded that the mound had been used by several generations of ancient man who once occupied Hare's Landing. Therefore, the large burial mound was a very important find. It showed that Hare's Landing was occupied and abandoned several times in its history.

Finding the more modern history of Hare's Landing has been very difficult. I believe we can assume that the landing was purchased by a Mr. Hare in the Georgia land lottery of around 1843. Perhaps, none of the Hare's came to the area to work the land. Or, perhaps they did but when they passed on, the farm they had created fell back into time.

Hare's is on a map published in 1900s, but on one list of landings for the steamboat era, there is no mention of it. However, when consulting an older book of steamboat landings, Hare's is on this one from 1868.

Next, we know that this land was once owned by the Stewart Lumber Company. Here existed a sawmill and a turpentine still called Whaley's Mill. Also, this is where Log Landing existed. Here, steamboats would dock and be loaded with logs and turpentine for the trip down river to the Gulf of Mexico. The time frame for this would take us into more modern times, around the 1920s.

A map published in the early 1960s, shows Hare's as the ranger station. From this I think we can conclude that when Lake Seminole was formed the wildlife rangers took over Hare's Landing.

History Keeps Repeating - Trail's End Resort

Just up river from what once was Hare's Landing and is now a Wildlife Management Area Landing, is Trail's End Resort. This was once the home of Butler's Ferry where freight and passengers loaded to travel the Chattahoochee and go on down to the Apalachicola River to Florida and then on down to the Gulf Coast.

Trail's End has a unique place in the history of the Lake Area. It seems to always have been the sight of a lot of activity, a meeting area on the shores of the Chattahoochee River.

Walking through the woods which separate the new cabins of Trail's End Resort from the ancient ribbon of water, this area's place in history involves when it's boundaries extended out, beyond where they exist today. This land was the site of docks for steamboats and ferries.

Turning back the pages of time, we enter the age of when the early families came to the area and established large beautiful plantations. Names like the Saunders, the Drakes and the Faircloths were very prominent then. Also at this time, the Turnage family came to the area. They turned their portion of land into a very lucrative ferry and landing business. They were the first recorded owners of what is now Trail's End Resort and much of the surrounding area.

The forefathers of the family were very adventurous and colorful. First to arrive here, Emanuel Turnage was born in 1831, in North Carolina. It is told that he left home as a teenager when his father sold his pony. He then headed South and in 1850, settled on the Chattahoochee River. He first lived in Jackson County, Florida, for several years before settling on the Georgia side of the River.

Legend tells us that Emanuel had several children, two with his first wife, whose name is unknown. These children were William and Susanna.

After the death of their mother, the children were raised by Emanuel's wife's relatives in South Florida.

Emanuel then married Rebecca Sellers in 1854. They then moved to the Georgia side and together they had eight children. Daniel was one of these.

Emanuel bought many acres of land along the Chattahoochee River. He farmed on most of these. However, he also realized the potential for the success of a ferry business that would connect the southwest corner of Georgia, which at this time was Decatur County, to Jackson County in Florida. Therefore, sometime around 1874, he started this venture and constructed his ferry and steamboat dock at the end of what is now Georgia State Route 253, (Spring Creek Road).

Emanuel's sense for business served him well. His ferry landing became a very popular crossing. It was the only ferry for miles around with the one up at Neal's Landing being the other. Also, the steamboats of this time carried passengers and cargo up as far as Columbus, Georgia, on the Chattahoochee and up to Bainbridge, Georgia, on the Flint River.

Turnage Ferry was also centrally located between the cities of Bainbridge, Georgia, Marianna in Florida, and Pensacola, also in Florida. These were the major places of this decade for the Chattahoochee River provided the most important north/south thoroughfare in this area as it connected southwest Georgia with the gulf port of Apalachicola.

Another plus for the Turnage's business was that there was a large stand of timber readily available. Emanuel provided this wood for fuel for the steamboats.

Also, at this time, no railroad was close by so Turnage Ferry and Landing was the major center for farmers to ship their cotton and other products to market. The ferry and landing was very popular with shipping companies who printed flyers with passenger fares from Turnage Ferry and Landing to the other ports on the three river system.

Emanuel ran his ferry until his death on March 25, 1912. It was then that his son, Daniel, bought most of his father's farmland as well as the Turnage Ferry and Landing from all of the other heirs. Daniel farmed and operated the ferry for several more years. Then in 1923, he sold the Turnage business to L.C. Butler. The business became known as Butler's Ferry and Landing.

The ferry business wasn't as busy as it was in its early days. However, there were still many folks who wanted to go across the Chattahoochee River in this manner. The Butlers continued to operate this business until around the 1940s.

A story that is told about the ferry landing is about several thieves who had stolen money from a store which was located farther down on Spring Creek Road. They ran from the scene of the crime on down State Route 253 (Spring Creek Road).

However, when they arrived at Butler's Ferry, they were caught as the ferry was on the Florida side of the river.

After World War II, the property in and around what is now included in the Trail's End land lease was part of the legacy of families like the Drakes, the Saunders, and Sam Fairchild. They had created large, majestic farms with cows and horses and hogs roaming free in the woodlands. Their trees were now being used for timber and turpentine instead of fuel for steamboats.

Then, in 1957, the lake was backed up. It flooded the land on which these families worked. It came up and flooded the woods. There were many low places where small ponds existed. Now with the impounded water straining for space, these low lands increased and became miniature lakes. Swamps popped up. No one knew for sure how it would be when it all ended. At Trail's End, things would never be the same. No longer was it located on the shores of the Chattahoochee River.

To make it more accessible, the Army Corps. of Engineers cut through a channel from the Chattahoochee River and joined it to an existing lagoon. They dredged this and put in a concrete landing. Thus was the beginning of the Trail's End Landing as we know it today. Now, all that remains of where the ferries and steamboats use to dock is a tiny scrap of land near the entrance to Trail's End's channel. The old access road is now under the backed up waters of the Chattahoochee River.

The first person to lease this area from the Corps. of Engineers was Ellison Dunn. He called this his place in the sun, Dunn's Landing. Dunn had a large dream for this area. It was to be a great stopping place. Camping, fishing, hunting, all would be easily available.

First, the marina was constructed. Covered docks were put in place along one shore of the lagoon. Next, came a store where bait and tackle and food and boating necessities could be bought. This store has since burned down, but the concrete slab on which it was built exists as the foundation for one of the new cabins. Also, part of it is a patio.

There is a small motel that sets back from the lagoon. No one knows for sure who built it. Most likely, it was the Dunns.

The Dunns ran their business until in the mid-1960s. This is when Bill and Mary Turner became the owners. They also are believed to have been the ones to call this landing, Trail's End.

During this time, the Turner's kept up the structures which Dunn had built. They did add one thing, a small dock on the opposite shore of the lagoon, away from the marina. This is still there.

The next owners of record are Myrtle and Vestor Towns who were there in 1975. They too, made their mark in Trail's End history. They were famous for the breakfasts which Myrtle would cook to treat the guests on the weekends. She did this in what is the large middle room of the motel.

Next were Steve and Patsy Hancock. They were owners in the late 1980s, up until 1993. For several years, under their ownership, Trail's End was a booming business. This is attributed to a police officer named Tom Griffin. He started the tradition of having occasional community picnics. He barbecued hogs, featured music, singing, and dancing. Also, it was not uncommon to have spontaneous fish fries for everyone in the campground.

People came from everywhere to vacation at Trail's End. Big boats would journey down from Atlanta to dock there. Here they found peace with nature and the southern hospitality which southwest Georgia is famous for. However, all came to an end when Steve went to Iraq in Desert Storm.

The next owners were Hank and Penny Girot. They ran the landing from the mid-1990s, to 2006. While they were the proprietors, the Girots revived the tradition of spontaneous fish fries. They also had crab boils cooked in New Orleans style by Hank, who was born and raised in the Big Easy.

Their ownership also saw the fire which burned down the old store. They installed a trailer which they used for a store as well as an eatery where you could get hamburgers, hot dogs and homemade chili.

Then, in 2006, Lucas Stewart purchased Trail's End Marina and Campground. Once again, these old grounds underwent great change. First is the name change to Trail's End Resort. New modern log cabins popped up and a new store and eatery has been constructed. The motel was radically changed and the docks had been updated.

Also, a houseboat community has been added at the foot of what remains of the old road to the Chattahoochee River.

From Heydays To Ghost Town-Parramore's Landing

Our area has the remarkable talent to remake itself! The history on our rivers is one of birth, decline, then once again, rebirth. The launch area known as Parramore's Landing exemplifies this cycle.

When seen now, there isn't much evidence that this was the site of three steamboat landings and many lumber related businesses. For it is even said that Parramore's was the site of ancient burial mounds. Since it is located across the Chattahoochee River from where a very large deposit of ancient pottery and bones were found, it is possible that it, too, was the home of significant burial mounds.

The discoveries were said to have been called the Alday Pond Mounds. It is told that they were just like the others found around the lower Chattahoochee River. It may be true, even though when going through the records of the archeological digs that took place in the early 1900s, and then in 1946, Parramore's was not mentioned. This may be because the Alday Pond Mounds were believed to have been ruined by the cultivation and planting of crops through the 1800s, and 1900s, the booming days for the agriculture business in this area. This means that they could have been gone when the formal digs took place.

Back in the 1600's, many Indians came to this area for the great hunting and fishing. The Spanish also came trying to claim the area for their country.

Parramore's presents another possibility. It may have been the site of the trading post which is mentioned in the diary of Rebecca Sherwood, the adopted daughter of trading post magnet, William Panton, owner of the Panton-Leslie Trading Company. Rebecca wrote of traveling up the Chattahoochee River to establish a post. She said she visited an Indian settlement that was north of the village known as Fairchild. Since Parramore's is about three miles above Fairchild, she may have been there working on setting up a store in this place.

Parramore's could have been the very place where Rebecca introduced coffee to the area and held gatherings for women where they worked on the goods that they made to be traded for other items. All of this was in the early 1700s.

The recorded Indian leader at Parramore's in 1763, is said to have been a Perryman. The Perrymans were a large family of Creek Indians who became the main driving force in the mid to late 1700s.

Up until 1821, most of the land along the rivers was occupied by Indians. However, the first American settlers had begun to drift in. They were mostly farmers who built their homes from the giant pines they found here. They tilled the land, planted crops and carved out a life for themselves.

Eventually, in what is now the area of Parramore's, a small community known as Owens Settlement began to thrive. It grew large enough to be the only place on the lower Chattahoochee River to have enough settlers for the mail ferry to stop. This was wonderful for the people because now they could communicate with their families.

However, the Civil War interrupted the settlement of this landing. After the War was over, Owens came out of its sleep and once again sprang to life. It yawned, stretched and started on the road to become a thriving community. By 1870, it had established itself as a very popular steamboat landing. The call of the boat whistle was heard echoing across the waters of the Chattahoochee River for miles as they made their way to this very busy landing. The community was renamed after the family who now owned the land, the Parramores.

The year 1875, saw this once tiny community add a third boat landing. This made this virgin area the largest landing on the Chattahoochee River at this time.

Up on the river banks, the farms were thriving, too. The importing and exporting of crops became a big business. Most popular was cotton and tobacco, which grew with lush abandon in the fields. Several large farms also planted and had good luck with sugar cane. All of these items were in high demand up in Columbus, Georgia, and all the way down to Apalachicola, Florida.

Local trees provided excellent lumber as well as turpentine. These were flourishing commodities at this time. Most of the turpentine was manufactured by the Watt's Turpentine Still.

The expansion continued and by 1890, Parramore's had grown large enough to have a post office. Then by 1900, there were five stores in town, a one room school house, a cotton gin, a sawmill a blacksmith shop and a grist mill. All of these activities provided jobs and wealth for the local residents.

At this time, the Oak Grove Church was built. Most community functions centered around this popular gathering place. Eventually, two more churches were constructed. The population grew and grew until it numbered in the thousands. Many older residents tell of large dances held on a wooden floor constructed at the Lawson Farm.

In 1905, the town was at its peak. However, what local residents did not realize was that the town was beginning to decay. It was inching closer and closer to looming disaster. The crop yield was dwindling each year as the nutrients were being sucked out of the ground. This was especially evident in the cotton crops. Everything was being taken and nothing was given back in return. The very farming that provided life was now in a slow death.

However, the flu epidemic of 1918, caused a fast and devastating decline in the population. The Parramore area as well as others along the rivers were ravaged by this killer. As the towns grew smaller, the cemeteries became larger as families buried their loved ones who were the victims of this epidemic. As if all of this suffering was not enough, the Great Depression came and life was very difficult.

As a result of all of these disasters, the 1920s, saw the boat traffic on our rivers virtually disappear. By now the railroad had a large foothold and was taking over the transportation of cargo and passengers. The once welcome sound of the steamboat's whistle no longer called out. At Parramore's, the now unused boat landings rotted away. The town itself slowly sagged and then succumbed to time.

The only industry to keep going was that of making turpentine. This hung on until World War II. Many men and women left the river and never returned. Eventually, Parramore's became a ghost town. Now the town, the homes, the stills are all gone. All that remains are the stories, the Owens Bellview Church and the cemeteries where the early pioneers sleep.

However, all did not completely die for a restaurant and campground came into being. It provided many fond memories, especially of its catfish dinner. Starting in the 1950s, Parramore's was the place to eat. During its heyday, it would fill to overflowing with Friday and Saturday diners along with the Sunday afternoon crowd. People came from everywhere to eat and enjoy the friendly, relaxed Southern atmosphere and dine with the view of the sparkling waters of the slough that passed by the restaurant windows. Diners would walk up the gradual hill to the restaurant's door to join those in the large room full of laughter and stories of fishing fun. The tasty aroma of catfish and hush puppies would engulf them.

Along with the restaurant, Parramore's had a popular campground. The large, shaded field provided many areas for setting up a tent or parking a trailer. It was once full of vacationers, now it is taken over by ghosts. Even though the area is now abandoned, the laughter still lingers in the air of the sad and sagging building. Ethereal figures float between imaginary tables going to and from a salad bar that now consists of dirt and plaster pieces.

Despite this sad site, Parramore's is still a very welcoming landing. Picnicking was and still is very popular here. Tables up on platforms still grace the shoreline of the slough. Each has a stove for cooking those hot dogs or hamburgers for you are more than welcome here.

No Stranger To Tragedy - Neal's Landing

Many of the old landings have been drowned. However, up the Chattahoochee River is the site of Neal's Landing, which has existed for a very long time, way before Lake Seminole. Back in the early 1800s, this was the site of a Creek Indian village and a very decisive Indian battle. Descendants of original residents say that Neal's Landing has been there as long as they can remember. However, it may not always have been called Neal's. A 1906, map does not show the name Neal's but Steam Mill Landing. No matter the name, it was always a very popular crossing.

In the early days of the steamboat, it was the sight of warehouses, a hotel and a store. A high volume of business was transacted here, both passenger and freight.

Neal's Landing also has a unique history, different from all the others because of the many deadly disasters which took place here. During the time of the steamboat, Neal's was the sight of at least three happenings in which passengers died. Then, when it was used as a ferry landing there were two more deaths. There may have been many others that were not recorded or remembered.

One of the earliest of the fatal disasters occurred in 1842, when the steamboat *General Harrison* went down. The Chattahoochee River had been a very angry strip of water when the *General Harrison* was making its way down to the Apalachicola River. The 184 ton vessel had just recorded another rise in the water which made the total to be around 50 feet.

On board the *General Harrison*, its captain decided to go just a little farther down stream to Neal's. Here he would tie up and wait for the river to subside. The paddle-wheeler may have over extended its boilers while trying to navigate the churning currents because it met an untimely end when it exploded, killing three men.

Another early disaster at Neal's Landing was the fire that sank the two ton steamboat *Eagle*. On June 29, 1854, a crewman was taking a walk on deck at around two in the morning. He discovered a fire raging amongst the cotton bales in the aft section near the paddlewheel. Attempts to put out the fire were unsuccessful. Six men lost their lives, two were crew men and four were slaves, all of which burned to death.

Another recorded sinking was that of the *City of Eufaula* which lived a short but glorious life. She was launched in 1912, on a bright sunny day in Apalachicola. Mrs. H.A. Daniels broke a bottle of Mumm's extra dry champagne on the steamboat's newly constructed hull. Slowly, gracefully, the *City of Eufaula* slipped into the warm waters of the Gulf of Mexico.

Under tow, she was brought up to Columbus, Georgia, where her construction was finished. The *City of Eufaula* was shiny, her hull still unstained from the cypress tinted waters of the rivers.

She met her untimely end at Neal's Landing. Here on February 11th, 1921, she caught fire. The flames burned the moorings lines and the boat with forty-five people on board were all at the mercy of the untamed Chattahoochee River. The boat burned as she floated down stream where she then succumbed to the will of the water. Miraculously, no one lost their life.

A few years later, Neal's Landing was sold to E. R. Ward of Iron City. He operated a ferry there until 1927. This is when the infamous Swinging Bridge was constructed over the Chattahoochee River by Austin Brothers Bridge Company of Austin, Texas. It was the only true suspension bridge south of the Mason-Dixon Line.

Constructed of wood and wire cable, it was anchored onto the banks on either side of the Chattahoochee River. The bridge, which spanned more than 600 feet, was said to have been one of the most beautiful structures in this section of the United States at this time.

Placed into service in August of 1927, it was 80 feet above the Chattahoochee River and was quite scary to cross. It was a true trembler because when trucks would go over, it would actually bounce and dance in response. This action increased with age as the cables were stretched. Just watching it was an experience.

Even though it was plagued by all of this movement, there were no records of accidents happening on the bridge. Nonetheless, in 1953, the Swinging Bridge was judged to be unsafe. This is when work began on the present bridge.

The new one was to be known as the Herman Tallmadge Bridge and would be built by Scott Construction Company of Thomasville. However, in the time between tearing down the old bridge and finishing the new bridge, a ferry was placed into service to take people across the Chattahoochee.

Ramps for the ferry were a little downstream from where the Tallmadge Bridge is today. The ramp on the Florida side is the boat launching ramp today. This was the original approach for the ferry on the Florida side.

This temporary ferry was to make it easier for residences to cross the river. Without it, they would have had to travel far up stream to what is now the Alaga Bridge, better known as the Highway 84 bridge.

In the four months the ferry was in operation, it proved to be more dangerous than the Swinging Bridge. The ferry sank twice and was the scene of two deaths. This accident occurred because the brakes on a vehicle that contained two men failed. Consequently, they drove off the deck of the ferry and into the swift current of the Chattahoochee River. Unable to escape, they went down in the car.

The ferry operated until 1957, when the present bridge was completed.

It All Began With Indian Canoes – Fairchild Landing

Wooded and overgrown, Fairchild Landing hides many secrets. The cool, dark earth has covered over the evidence of ancient Indians as well as a Creek Indian village.

Before modern man a came, Fairchild was on a 20 foot high bluff made of red clay, yellow sand and dark, rich earth. The area was covered with large trees and dense undergrowth. The ground was hardly visible, except for scattered small, cultivated plots and a few trails.

Later, in time and because of the impending construction of the Woodruff Dam, an expedition was formed to investigate the land that would be covered by the water of what was to be Lake Seminole.

This archeological dig was one and a half miles north and west of the crossroads of what is now Ned Alday River Road and Fairchild Landing Road. This parcel of land was owned by Bartow Saunders before the government bought it. Having never been cleared of vegetation, it was wild and largely inaccessible woodlands. However, the terrain was familiar to the local hunters and fishermen.

When the Smithsonian Institute took over the exploration, many ancient disposal pits and mounds were found. Most contained many pieces of broken pottery, charcoal, flint and animal bone fragments. So much pottery was found! This pottery was not only abundant but it was of a new, undiscovered style and an unknown stamping which was completely intact. So important was this find that the pottery was named Fairchild Pottery.

Some of these treasured artifacts were found in a part of what was a very uneven terrain. Some large deposits were uncovered from dirt only 5 feet below the surface, while other pieces were found only 14 inches down. The most productive mound was 36 feet by 27 feet. Many animal bones, flint fragments, pottery and charcoal were unearthed.

It was the Creek Indians that gave Fairchild its name. History tells us that this village was named after the Indian chief, Fair Child. His was a peaceful tribe that worked hard at farming and raising animals, growing corn and other vegetables as well as harvesting honey. Cattle and hogs were found in abundance grazing on their land.

An Indian legend tells this story of the meeting of Chief Fair Child's daughter, Mary, and the world wide traveler and river pirate, William Bowles.

A rich soldier of fortune, Bowles tried three times to overthrow the Spanish government in Cuba. However, each time he was caught and put in a dungeon in Havana, but all three times he escaped. The last time he left Cuba, he made his way to Apalachicola, Florida. From there, he followed the Apalachicola River, stopping at each village along the way. These tribes told him about the beautiful Indian princess, Mary, who lived at Fair Child. When he met her, he found that all the stories were true, not an exaggeration.

The couple fell in love and they were married. Shortly afterwards, they left the village and traveled down the Chattahoochee River, on to the Apalachicola River, then on down to the Gulf of Mexico. This was in 1800.

Their union produced one son that we know of named, Little Willy. He became an important leader when he helped his people during the Trail of Tears migration to Oklahoma. Ultimately, Mary went to on this journey and died at this reservation.

Bowles was captured and once again was sent back to Cuba. He died in a prison in Havana in 1805.

As time passed, the inhabitants of the Fairchild area changed. White men took over the territory. The Saunders family, the Drake family and the Faircloth family became large plantation owners here.

Progress came in the form of a steamboat landing. The plantations and the small farms were joined together by the logging and turpentine industries. A still site was built near the crossroads at Ned Alday River Road and Fairchild Landing Road. This is believed to have been started around 1870.

By most logging mills and turpentine stills, booming communities existed and Fairchild was no exception. It had a post office with John T. Saunders as post master, a school and a cotton gin along with a large commissary where residents could buy all they needed. There also were houses for those who worked at Fairchild.

From this bustling community, many products were shipped by the steamboats which stopped at the landing. Tupelo honey, resin and turpentine spirits, timber and cotton were the chief exports.

A story about the first turpentine still built there tells us that it was made of wood and sat on the ground. Even so, as stills are, it was very flammable. Inevitably, it caught fire and burnt until is was just a pile of ashes. After this, a two story brick building was erected. It is recalled that a turpentine still was in existence sometime around 1915. This still remained operational until sometime in the 1970s. Some remains of this structure are said to still be there.

Another historical story tells of a small, very old cemetery containing 14 graves believed to be that of the Faircloth family members. One stone is legible. It is engraved with the name James Wilson, born January 31, 1780, and died 1850.

Eventually, a part of the Saunders/Faircloth plantation became the 225 acre Fairchild State Park.

What Time Has Forgotten - Confederate Naval Yard

In what is now a grassy field, on the east side of the Chattahoochee River, there once existed a Confederate Naval Yard. There are no physical remains of the ship yard and sawmill, even the exact area is uncertain. Still, memories are lurking everywhere because it did play an important part in the drama of the Civil War.

As the War between the States went on, the Chattahoochee River became more important. Partly, this was because the Confederate Army had placed an arsenal in Chattahoochee, Florida, a small town which is now on the east side of the Woodruff Dam. Because of this location, it was a top priority target of the Union Army. Attempting its takeover was the first military action in the three rivers' area.

Also, the Union Army had already begun blockading key supply ports in the Gulf of Mexico. One of the important ports was that of Apalachicola. Therefore, getting supplies to this city and then on up the river was getting very difficult.

However, up on most of the Chattahoochee River, it was business as usual. The steamboats that were on the river at this time remained there and did so for the duration of the War because the Confederacy kept control of the river traffic. However, without new supplies coming in, the schedule soon dwindled.

When the blockade began, it was the steamboat, *Montgomery,* that spread the news up the Chattahoochee River to Columbus, Georgia. This brought the war to the doorstep of southwest Georgia. The need for ships that were blockade runners, specially equipped steamships, was now a real necessity.

To answer this call, Chief Engineer James Warner, and his assistant, Confederate Navy Lt. Augustus McLaughlin, negotiated a contract with David S. Johnston of Saffold, a tiny Georgia town, for the construction of the wooden gunboat, *CSS Chattahoochee.* She was to be 130 feet long, 30 feet at the beam and required 2 feet of draft. She was to have 2 engines and 2 propellers.

The *Chattahoochee's* armament was to consist of 6 guns, 1 forward, 1 pivotal gun aft and 4 on the broadsides. The forward gun was to be a 32 pound rifled cannon. The aft gun was to be the deadly, 9 inch Dahlgren. The broadside cannons were to be 6 inches and classed as 32 pounders. Seventy-eight men were required to man these guns and some 22 others for the rest of the duties aboard ship such as boatswains, paymaster and surgeon.

The reason that Saffold, Georgia, was chosen was because it was about in the geographic middle, from Apalachicola and Columbus. Also there was an existing sawmill and an ample supply of timber already in existence that was capable of cutting 5000 board feet a day.

The *CSS Chattahoochee,* was one of eight ships constructed specifically for river defense, but the only one built at Saffold. The others that came to defend the rivers were built as far away as South Carolina.

The contract for the *Chattahoochee,* was signed on October 19th, 1861. She was to be completed in 120 days, sometime around February 19th, 1862.

Meanwhile, the blockade forces off the city of Apalachicola kept growing, reinforcing the need for the shallow draft vessel that was being built.

By the end of 1861, the pressure from the blockade seemed to have eased and all military action in this area was, on a whole, sporadic. However, because of the lack of cargo, the river traffic had decreased significantly signaling that Confederate control had weakened.

Meanwhile, at the ship yard in Saffold, the completion date for the war ship had come and gone. It was written in the company log that "she (the *Chattahoochee*) is ready to plank up and in one month will be ready for the water." This put the target launch date to sometime in March.

The high water that had plagued the winter months, continued into that spring causing the *Chattahoochee's* construction site to be under water for several days at a time hindering the progress.

By now, Johnston was behind in his contract. Contributing to his woes was a labor shortage. The following ad appeared in March in the *Columbus Sun,* "Hands wanted at the Confederate Navy Yard located on the Chattahoochee River at Saffold, Georgia, to build gunboats."

Some 20 carpenters, joiners and caulkers were employed and made exempt from military duty. Also during the month of March, Johnston supposedly had contracted to build two more gunboats. At the same time, William and Adam Saffold had allegedly contracted to build these same two gunboats. All were to be larger and more heavily armed than the *Chattahoochee*. However, no trace of these contracts was ever found nor were the boats ever built.

Finally, in the summer of 1862, the gunboat, *CSS Chattahoochee*, was completed. She was now ready to enter the Civil War on the Chattahoochee River and patrol the river to the Forks area, then down the Apalachicola River. Finally, the *Chattahoochee*, was doing what she was built for.

She stopped off at Blountstown, Florida, on the Apalachicola River, to take on supplies for the trip farther down to the Gulf of Mexico. On the day she was to depart, there was an argument in the engine room. How much water was needed to be maintained in the boilers was being disputed. The pilot started the engine, which pumped water to the main boiler. However, when this water reached the boiler, it exploded killing 14 men. Some crew members were scalded by the hot, falling rain, while others feared more explosions from the powder magazines and jumped overboard.

The mighty war ship began to sink and the abandon ship order was given. In the aftermath of the tragedy, the wounded were placed on the muddy shores of the river and later taken to a nearby cotton gin.

The sad remains of the *Chattahoochee* were towed to the right bank of the Apalachicola River and the bow hauled on land while the stern sat in 12 feet of water.

David Johnston of the Saffold Navy Yard came to the rescue and took charge. He raised the wreck. Then took the most valuable parts, mostly her metal boilers and rudders, on up to the Columbus Naval Yard where they would be rebuilt. The hull went in Saffold for repairs. Once ready, the hull was towed up to Columbus and the *Chattahoochee* was once again made whole.

While repairs were going on, the Confederate Navy planned a major assault against the Union blockade with the *Chattahoochee* playing a big part. When she once again joined the War, she did not have her full complement of guns and her boilers were still in deplorable condition. Nevertheless, she set her course for down river and to fight in the battle.

The *Chattahoochee* did well until she ran aground near Eufaula. Eight men from the *Chattahoochee* rowed down stream to the Saffold Navy Yard for the supplies to repair her.

Thankfully, the water on the Chattahoochee River rose and the gunboat was able to make her way downstream to her assigned destination, Chattahoochee, Florida. From there the *Chattahoochee* proceeded down the Apalachicola River to just below Blountstown, to the area known as the Narrows, then on to the city of Apalachicola, on the Gulf of Mexico.

Both the boat and crew arrived safely in Apalachicola. Here the *Chattahoochee* spent several months fighting at the blockade. She made a very good account of herself and was fiercely fighting when once again her boilers caused her to be towed away. Upset and forlorn, the warship needed to go all the way to the Columbus Navy Yard for her repairs.

However, by this time, Sherman was trying to take over Atlanta. The *Chattahoochee's* 32-pound guns were taken there for its defense. Meanwhile, the Confederacy was still trying to break the Union blockade at Apalachicola.

In early 1865, the Union Army broke through the Confederate defenses and entered the city of Columbus, where the *Chattahoochee* was being refitted. To keep her from enemy hands, the *Chattahoochee* was set on fire by her crew using 10 barrels of kerosene and slow burning matches.

Fleeing from the burning vessel, her crew sadly watched her demise. Slowly, with dignity, she drifted southward as if to return to the comfort and safely of Saffold, the place of her birth. However the valiant Confederate warship, *Chattahoochee*, did not make it that far, coming to rest at Race Path, 12 miles below Columbus.

In 1865, the War came to an end. In the aftermath, the *Chattahoochee's* boilers, engines and propellers were sold to be refitted on another steamboat. Thus ended the life of the gunboat built in Saffold, Georgia, at the Confederate Navy Yard.

GETTING TO KNOW SPRING CREEK

Of the three waterways involved in the construction of the Woodruff Dam, Spring Creek was the one most affected by the changes in the environment. She is fairly shallow with her sides spreading out over what once was marsh lands and swamp. It is this tendency that has made her vulnerable to exotic weed growth. Luckily, her channel markers show where her original course once was providing deeper water.

However, Spring Creek is more than just another pretty face. Shy, shallow and unassuming, it is the most seductive of the water ways that make up Lake Seminole.

She begins as a shiny trickle in northern Early County. She peaks around islands and skitters over stumps. She twists and turns and wiggles as she gains momentum, jumping over rocks and flirting with cypress knees and water grasses. Her water bubbles up from deep within the earth and teams with fish. She sparkles with the crystal clear springs. This pure, deep water exists all along her course.

Progressively, her scenery goes from beautiful to exceptional. Her banks have been the scene of much history and sadly, the water has covered most of this.

As Spring Creek gets closer to where she empties into Lake Seminole, she becomes very, very wide. No longer does she resemble the creek she was in the time before the dam. Then, in one final swoop, Spring Creek converges with the Flint River. Together, they have created an intriguing tapestry of green islands and shallow blue, brown waters.

A Brief Encounter With Spring Creek

There are many hidden secrets under the water of Spring Creek waiting to bubble up like the springs that comprise this waterway. Some of the legends that swirl around have to do with the Osuchi Indians. Herot's Rock, the Old Rock Bridge and the pictograph cave, all have contributed to colorful Indian lore.

Landings on Spring Creek were more numerous back before the Woodruff Dam. Those which still exist have different names. Oil Still Springs Landing was near the mouth of Spring Creek. What is now Rattlesnake Point was called Tobacco Patch Landing.

Before Reynolds Landing on the left hand side of the lagoon as you face north, was Lime Sink Slough. On the right hand side of the lagoon was Thursby Landing. Whittaker Landing used to be near where the paved road of County Road 123 makes a sharp 90 degree turn. Old Mill Landing was nestled between Whittaker's and present day Knights Landing which was then Rhodes Ferry Landing. Farther down from Knights was Joe Johnson Landing, then on up to the Spring Creek Powerhouse.

Spring Creek appears on an early Indian map as being called *Wecisy-Wan-Thlucco*. It was once a flourishing Indian village populated by the Osuchi tribe which came up here from Florida.

On a 1763 map, in a London records office, the banks of the Flint River are shown. Then, just above what is now Knights Landing, the map also shows a settlement with the walls of a fort around it. It is named Fort Cheskie, which was also believed to have been an Osuchi Indian settlement.

On a 1778 map, Spring Creek is simply called, the Springs.

Spring Creek was also mentioned on several maps of the area in the early 1800s. One settlement that is shown was that of Seminole Indians called *Wekivas*. It had a population close to 250 persons. Its chief was Menohamatha Hajo.

One map from around 1818, shows that the old Fort Scott Road once crossed Spring Creek in Miller County. This road entered Fort Scott near what was then called Oil Still Springs which was just up from the cut through to modern day Spring Creek Park Resort.

Ruled By Ghosts – Taking A Journey

There are many stories from the past that are a part of Spring Creek's charm. To learn of these we will take a journey from where Spring Creek and the Flint River join and go on up, as far as we can.

First, we will try to imagine Spring Creek as she was hundreds of years ago. Lets try to connect all of these islands into one land mass. In doing this, we can see where the low lying marsh lands once were.

Next, we pick out where once the boundaries of Spring Creek were. This is simple for the channel markers show us this path. Outside of them the water is riddled with stumps and tangled with water grasses.

Now we come upon White Springs, the site of an archeological excavation. Named for a very impressive size spring which is off of Sealy's Landing on the right near the Fort Scott Islands, White Springs is now under Lake Seminole. This ancient site, probably around 2000 years old, consisted of two small cooking pits and one large one, 8 feet wide by 15 feet long and 8 inches deep. These pits were on relatively high ground which overlooked the spring. Near the shoulder of the largest pit, archeologists found what proved to be the burial of an old woman. She was apparently a slave who had the misfortune of dying during meal preparation. A hastily dug two by two foot grave was chopped out of the ground next to the large fire pit. The body was then quickly crammed into the small spot. She had none of the accompanying items which were usually buried with the dead to make their journey into the afterlife more pleasant. Thus, the belief that she was a slave.

Next, we notice that the channel narrows. Then, on the right is an opening through the banks of Spring Creek. This leads to Buffalo Pond, the sight of a family tragedy. It seems that the youngest child contracted yellow fever. Then everyone got it. Sadly, the family perished. However, people were spread so far from each other that no one knew what had happened to them.

One day, while the Army Corps. of Engineers was digging a channel from Buffalo Pond to Spring Creek several headstones were unearthed. No one knew that this cemetery was there. The bodies had long been gone and just these unreadable headstones remained. Nonetheless, out of respect for those gone, the Corps. placed the head stones and the dirt from the graves farther up along the shoreline of Spring Creek.

Next, over on the right hand side is the legendary place called Herot's Rock. Amidst the gentle sway of the cattails and the chattering of the bull frogs, Indian women once sat up on this large rock and waited for their warriors to come home from hunting.

At one time, this rock was near the banks of the original Spring Creek and just a short distance from the Osuchi Indian village. Now the rock is in a shallow, grassy area, just off from a large house. Most of the time, Herot's Rock is covered by water but when the water is low you can float carefully in a canoe like boat to it.

Another historical sight is a little farther up from Herot's Rock, where there existed a cave. It, too, is on the right hand side where the banks of the Spring Creek are still high. Legend says that the Osuchi Indians once crawled through the long tunnel that led them to the inner chamber. Here, they hid from encroaching enemies. While there, they drew pictures on the cave walls that told of their tribal customs and what was happening to their culture. Sadly, all is under water now.

Still going up towards our destination, we come to the place where the Old Rock Bridge, sometimes called Swan's Bridge, was built by the Indians so that they could take their ponies across the creek and take advantage of the hunting grounds on the other side. This rock wall was near where the Nichols grist mill once stood. Here, the original creek was very narrow, making it an easy place to build a bridge.

This structure remained intact for quite a while. Some early residents used it after the Indians were gone. It is thought that after withstanding over a century of floods and swift currents, sometime in the early 1900s, it had been washed away. There are no remains.

Now, we need to stop and listen very closely. Do you hear them? People. They are laughing and talking. Their voices are echoing off of the high clay banks and are being bounced from tree to tree. In our time this area is called Ralph King Landing. However, in the past this site was referred to as Happy Hollow.

It has always been a cool, green meadow that stretches from down by the yellow power dam which is now visible up stream, past to where a high yellow-orange bank can be seen. This was THE place. People gathered here for picnics, family reunions and just plain fun.

To say that the area is beautiful would be an understatement. However, it does not look the same now. As we pass between the Spanish moss covered trees of Spring Creek, the vivid colors of the still steep cliffs become visible. We know all that is left are these aging and eroded banks.

Back in time, the banks of the creek were higher and much steeper. Erosion from rain and boat traffic have gouged them, scoured them and shrunk them down. Once you would have been able to jump off into the sparkling waters of Spring Creek.

Some added attractions were the many ropes that were attached to the tree limbs. From here, people could swing out over the cool, deep spring water, let go and fall into the green darkness below. Many think that half of the people in the area learned to swim here.

No sojourn up Spring Creek is complete without seeing the old Spring Creek Powerhouse and Dam. It is the king of the area. As the structure comes into view, try to imagine when the dam wall was still there and blocked off the water up stream to form Lake Decatur. This aging structure talks softly about a past that began when it was erected in 1920s. This powerhouse has seen many floods in its time. It has also seen many bridges come and go. Most remembered is a wooden bridge that allowed vehicles to pass over the water but not pass each other.

It is remembered too, as a great place to fish. Also, many residents recall being baptized in the shadow of the powerhouse.

Our eyes now travel to the bank across from the old power dam. This is where a Civilian Conservation Corps, a CCC camp, was located. This was during the Depression years of the 1930s.

We will stop here because going up farther is dangerous and is mostly frequented by canoers and kayakers.

The Path Barely There - Civilian Conservation Corps

Sometimes we don't realize it but the lake area has played an active role throughout our country's history. Perhaps this is because it is so peaceful and full of beauty that we get distracted and forget that we have had explorers, Indians and battles rage here.

However, during the 1930s, there was a Civilian Conservation Corps. camp on the shores of Spring Creek that existed just before the Spring Creek Powerhouse and Dam and just across the road from the restaurant, Pace's Fish Camp. The path is barely open now. The old buildings of the CCC camp are almost completely gone, but not the memories.

An off shoot of President Franklin Roosevelt's New Deal program to get the country out of the Great Depression, these camps improved the country's natural resources, and replanted forests which were quickly becoming decimated. The men worked in flood control, and were a part of a massive road building program. They also helped in the protection of the habitats of wildlife. To accomplish this, the program established most of the parks and recreation areas that we love to visit to this day.

For a man to be accepted into the Civilian Conservation Corps., he had to be between 18 and 25 years old. Those whose families had applied for state welfare were the first to be accepted.

In return for their work, the men were furnished with housing, clothing, food and medical services. At first, home was a large, canvas tent. However, as time went on, home became a comfortable barracks. Clothing which was given to each man started out as old Army uniforms but as with housing, this improved over time and became comfortable coveralls and shirts.

Their daily routine was similar to that of the Army and most of the men thrived under it. They awoke early for mess to the sound of a bugle. They ate meals at a certain time and went to bed at a certain time each day.

Every man had his own work responsibilities. On an average, men worked six days a week and had evenings and Sundays off.

Pay started at $30 a month with $25 sent home to the men's families. Gradually, this changed and the men could keep more of their money as more jobs became available for other family members.

Occasionally, the CCC members were called to help in emergencies such as fires, and floods. The men also learned many valuable skills like how to operate many types of heavy equipment such as bulldozers and dump trucks. Some men, who because of economics, did not get to go to school, even learned to write and do arithmetic while at the camp.

Here, at Spring Creek, the path to the camp is almost blocked by live oaks draped with Spanish moss. They all but obliterated where the site existed. Even the old wooden buildings, evidence that there was a camp, are gone. Nothing remains of this ghost town.

In its day, the camp was constructed from wood which was provided by the Stewart Lumber Company of Lela. At this time, the lumber company owned the land which became the Civilian Conservation Camp. The lumber to build the camp was either cut from the camp site or from the forest near the tiny town of Lela.

The camp had three long barracks. One went north and south with the others going east to west. The north to south building was a supply room, a kitchen and mess hall. The two east to west buildings were sleeping quarters.

The camp housed around 200 men. Most of these either came from Bainbridge or from the Birmingham, Alabama, area. Here, they mostly worked on flood and fire prevention. Most of the fire breaks that they constructed are still used to protect local forests. They planted to replenish the pine tree forests and to prevent soil erosion. They also sprayed to rid the area of mosquitoes because the incidence of malaria in our area was high.

Mostly by hand, they constructed roads, some of which are by the powerhouse and on west to Bowen Earnest Road. These men also placed telephone poles and cables through the camp, then on over through the woods and on out to Desser.

The men of the camp had fun, too. They loved to play baseball for recreation. This attracted many local men who also loved this sport. Young and old would come to watch or join in. This area is the source of many vivid memories. This grassy meadow was referred to as the Pit. Here locals would watch the men play baseball and they too, held their own games here. The camp ball field is still visible as a grassy meadow where there are no bushes or underbrush.

When I visited there were two buildings that still existed. One was leaning precariously to the right for the trees around it were very large and seemed to be trying to squeeze it into submission. This building was a maintenance shack. It was the place where the men came to work on the heavy equipment or gather the rakes and shovels needed to do the work for the day.

Farther down the path was another wooden structure almost obliterated by the trees and underbrush. It was full of the remnants of a by gone day. Bed springs, an old stove and a very sad mattress which bulged forth with life as many tiny mice called it home. Still standing up against a far wall was a well-worn, wooden cupboard. Beneath inches of dust and dirt were the remains of wood that still had a glossy shine.

Behind this frame building is a thick brick structure that once was a spring house or ice house. It, too, needed to have the extra support of surrounding trees as it clings to its upright position.

Farther away, and well hidden from sight are sad and falling brick chimneys that were a part of the living quarters.

The history of the camp continued after it was no longer used. For a short while it became a school when the one in Reynoldsville burned down. This was for the years 1943 to 1945. It also was used as a church camp.

Several local residents had memories of meeting the men who worked at the camp. They remembered how the men were always happy to see the young boys and would stop and talk to them for the children reminded them of home.

The men also held good natured boxing matches which were at the camp on Saturday nights. Others remembered when the camp was used as a school and they went to their junior and senior proms there.

From Hogs To A Marina - Spring Creek Park Resort

To say that the Woodruff Dam changed the landscape of the area is like saying the carrier, *USS Enterprise*, is just another boat. The change was enormous! However, some areas show the transformation more than others. One such place is Reynolds Landing also known as Spring Creek Park Resort. In our time, the edge of Reynolds Landing is about a half mile from where it originally existed.

In the beginning, Reynolds Landing was a very wild and untamed place as in this legend. In this area, women went down to the shores of Spring Creek to wash clothes. As they gathered there, the children ran and played and the women exchanged happenings. One day, while there alone, a woman and her child spotted a great bear. She feared for her life and that of her small child. Carefully, she picked the toddler up and made her way through the woods hiding behind the massive pines until she was back in their cabin. This day, they had survived the bear.

Before the water was backed up, the Spring Creek area was covered with lots of small ponds. The peaceful lagoon where Reynolds Landing and now Spring Creek Park Resort exists was once just a low spot where hogs rooted. The animals would dig all summer as far down as they could go to reach water to cool themselves in the heat. When the clearing crew came, they made it a little deeper and cleared out some of the timber.

The Reynolds Landing of old was about one half mile out toward where the channel for Spring Creek is now. It also was down a little farther toward Sealy's Landing. Where the original Reynolds Landing existed is now under the waters of Lake Seminole.

The Reynolds family owned this large track of land which was thick with huge pine trees, ones which supplied a lot of turpentine and good lumber. However, when the Army Corps. of Engineers took over, they bought the land along with the timber rights. When the clearing crews came they sawed out the trees that could be used for timber. Sadly, that beautiful woodland that the Reynolds family owned slipped under the backed up waters of Spring Creek in the late 1950s. Eventually, the Corps. cut through the land and connected all of the small ponds, creating a deep channel that enters the peaceful lagoon where Reynolds Landing is situated.

Even with all of the clearing, when the water backed up, it was like flooding the woods. People would get lost quite easily. Sometimes they didn't make it back before dark. When it was suspected that someone was lost, men would go out and search for them.

Another hazard then, as now, were those stumps. When the crews cleared the land they did not cut the trees down to the ground. Then as now, you had to be careful not to put a hole in your boat.

The land that was spared by the flood waters became Reynolds family land by a temporary one year lease from the Corps. Since most of the timber was taken, Ken Reynolds and his brothers decided to try operating a boat landing.

Before the water was backed up, not many of the visiting boaters ventured from Spring Creek to the Flint River. Remember, the two didn't meet until farther down, past where Sealy's Landing is now. Also, most people would have had to row the distance. Some had small motors but didn't make the time consuming journey.

Ken and his brothers felt that renting boats would be a great way for people to experience the fishing on Spring Creek. Back then, money was hard to come by. Most people didn't own their own boats. The rental boats provided a way for them to enjoy going out onto the water.

They started with 20 boats and found that these were always rented. With the venture being successful, at the end of the year, they bid on the land and purchased it. This was in 1957.

After a couple of years, Ken bought his brothers' share of the business. He then increased his fleet to 100 boats. He set up a small, wooden shack with just enough cover to get in out of the rain. From this place, he rented his boats and motors. Usually, all were rented by mid morning. Sometimes people would bring their own motors and mount them on the Reynolds' boats.

As the waters of Lake Seminole rose, Ken Reynolds had to move his business farther and farther back until it was situated where it is now. Eventually, he replaced his original wooden shed with the present block building. Along with being the rental area, he added a restaurant. Reynolds became well known for his hot dogs and hamburgers. Later, came gas pumps and the motel. This is believed to be the oldest motel on the Seminole County side of Lake Seminole. Reynolds ran this business for many years before he sold it.

In his years at the landing, Reynolds had many adventures. One which remains vivid is the time lightning struck a houseboat. It was during one of southwest Georgia's famous storms when the lightning streaked down from the sky and set the boat on fire. Both the boat and the dock were burned. If you want to picture this in your mind, the burned section of the dock stood out on the right hand side of the main deck across from the fish cleaning shelter.

There have been several owners in the past. However the current owners, Steve and Reed Rognstad, have made several improvements in the years they have been there which includes remodeling the restaurant now known as R's Café and the other, The Oyster Bar. They also host the successful Annual Lake Seminole Festival.

A Haven In The Past - Jackson's Oven

Near the Spring Creek shoreline, just past Knights Landing, there once stood a structure known as Jackson's Oven. Made of stone, brick and mud, this building was believed to have existed from sometime in the early 1800s, when the Indians roamed the woods and settlers were few. In thinking about this structure, it brings the idea that it must have been something like constructing the pyramids. Building this mystery room must have taken a lot of time and a lot of man power to achieve it because it had to be done with primitive tools.

First, the rock had to be broken and then dug out from the banks of Spring Creek before the walls could be made. The Indians probably had to use shovels and picks made from wood instead of metal implements because they were rare. Also, the Indians would not have had easy access to them.

Even so, when the room was finished, it was quite large with its measurements being 9 feet going north to south and 15 feet going east to west. Its walls were about 5 feet high and 3 feet thick.

There was one doorway to enter and that was 28 inches by 72 inches. Like a split level house, from the foyer, there were stone steps led the way down two and a half feet below the surrounding ground and into the main body of the stone structure. Here, there was a large, brick chimney.

The uses for this place were speculated upon and there are many theories on what the use for this structure was. Opinions also vary on the timing of this stone room. Some we know are legends and some can be true. It is thought to have been the work of Indians, but the Spaniards were in this neighborhood for several hundred years too. However, the where and the way it was constructed leans towards it being the work of the Indians. They would have made sure that a building like this would have been near a running stream and on as level ground as was possible. The running water needed by the tribe would have come from Spring Creek.

It was customary that at the head of a town, the Indians would construct a small round building. Then they would place guards inside. From the location and the design of the structure, it could have been a guard house.

Many other uses suggested have been that it was once a sweat lodge, or an oven or kiln for firing pottery. However, this probably was not a use because having this amount of heat in the chimney would have caused the mud to crumble. It could not have stood this heat.

Mostly, and the most probable, is that it had been a storehouse that protected the food supplies for the Indians from the heat and the sun. Maize, fruits, nuts, roots, fish, alligator, dog, deer and other dried meats may have been stored here.

From stories told by residents, the room was first discovered in 1900. At this time, it was not in a good state of preservation. Since it was constructed out of flint and limestone and cemented with some kind of mud type substance, it had crumbled and broke through time.

A popular story is that inside its stone walls, General Jackson's Army cooked their meals while they were camped here on their way to Fort Scott. However, its location is too far away from the objective to have been used by the garrison at Fort Scott.

It is also thought that it was a place where Confederate soldiers sought shelter while on their way back to their homes. This is a very probable scenario as it would have provided these men the shelter that they truly needed.

There are no remains of Jackson's Oven now. At one time, there were bricks scattered around from its chimney. However, being broken and abandoned, residents took them and used them for their own chimneys.

A Place Lost To Time - Sealy Mansion

When the waters of Spring Creek were to be backed up, an extensive archeological dig took place. During this excavation, three prehistoric mounds were found on what was to become the Sealy Plantation. Archeologists discovered, to no one's surprise, that in ancient times, Spring Creek was a sportsman's paradise. The deep springs were clear waters providing an aquarium setting for fish and shellfish.

Even though the landscape had changed, the trained eye of the archeologist found evidences of hunting and fishing paths through the woods and along the banks of the creek. Eroded patches of shell deposits joined piles of animal bones. Turtle shells and pottery shards also were found along these paths.

With this evidence, the Sealy land was most likely a camping area as no human burials were found. One of the mounds was found by the mansion door. It contained a small collection of 15 pottery shards. Another mound was in a vegetable garden and still another out in the yard.

In more modern times, this area became one of the most popular landmarks, at the mouth of Spring Creek, close to where she joins the Flint River. Even though time did its best to erase the past, covering over the landmarks and blurring memories until just the legend is left, the story of the Sealy mansion lives on. Woven from the threads of fact and fiction, its stories have created a cloth of colorful hearsay to embellish the black and white truths.

It is believed that there was considerably more than 100 acres making up the plantation grounds. The original entrance was just off State Route 253, (Spring Creek Road), between where two ponds now exist. An iron gate and giant oak once provided landmarks for the entrance.

This road meandered by Cypress Pond, then over to Reynolds Landing. If you know where to look, you will see the remains of an old wooden bridge where it once crossed an embankment. From here the road bent toward the west by the manor house.

The shoreline of the estate was formed by Spring Creek, which at that time, was a narrow line, lazily making its way to where it blended with the Flint River. The Sealy estate was one of peaceful, plowed earth, and moist hungry land which waited for seeds to spring to life. Surrounding it were thick pine forests. Dark and cool, the trees stood with age old patience. The pines created woods which were teaming with game. They also provided turpentine and timber. Wandering on grassy knolls were Texas Longhorn cattle, grazing on the lush foliage and seeking shelter in the pines from the intense summer sun.

The plantation manor house was perched on the top of a grassy hill which now is the site of Sealy Circle. No one is sure when the house was built. It is speculated to have been around the 1880s. Residents who remember 1900, say the house was already there. Whether or not the Sealys were the original builders is not known, but they are believed to have been.

The house has been described as a two story mansion reminiscent of Tara in gone *With The Wind*. Its sturdy, white walls would reflect the wild crimson of the setting sun. Huge, Greek style columns effortlessly supported the great expanse of roof which covered the spacious verandah, providing cooling shade for the home's occupants.

A feature recalled by most is the circular shaped houseboat that was kept moored at the end of a dock. It resembled a giant life raft as it encircled one of the deep, blue springs for which Spring Creek is famous. The interior was made entirely of glass. A board walk was also part of the interior where guests who stayed aboard the houseboat could walk from their rooms and look down into the spring teeming with fish.

Now, the only evidence of the mansion that once existed, is the windmill that provided water for the house, standing like a metal knight in what was the former backyard. However, folklore does provide a reason for the fact that there is no evidence of the house. Sealy didn't feel income taxes were fair. Therefore, he did not pay them. Consequently, the government decided to take more of his land for back taxes. At the final stage of the trial, Sealy supposedly told the judge that no uninvited person was going to spend a moment in the house which he had built. Coincidentally, the house burned down that night. However it happened, there are no remains of the mansion and most people state that they do not remember anything of it after 1960.

Another story told enlightens us about an earlier court fight. When the water was backed up by the Jim Woodruff Dam, Mr. Sealy fought the flooding of the land in court. While the lawsuit was in progress, the trees were not allowed to be cut. However, the building of the dam went forward and the water came up and surrounded the trees and drowned the land. This is the reason that there are so many dead trees and stumps in the area of the Sealy Plantation.

Mr. Sealy had a reputation for being larger than life. He is remembered as being kind, generous, full of life and fun. A renowned land baron, Sealy was a sporting man who also possessed tons of business savvy. It is believed he owned an oil business, a cattle ranch, a farm and a hotel as well as the many acres he farmed in Seminole County.

A certain age group remembers Sealy's kindness to children. Because he was not able to drive, his chauffeur would bring him to the plantation. Local children would dot the roadway which he traveled and the car would stop and he always had candy for them along with a kind greeting and a hug. Also, he would invite children to the house for ice cream in a time when this was a rare commodity. Since the Sealy's ran a dairy and ferried their milk down the Apalachicola River, then over to Panama City, in Florida, they always had cream to make this treat.

Two occupants of the house that local people remember were a Cajun couple, Jace the butler and his wife, Ginny the house keeper. The exotic aroma of good cooking was always evident around the Sealy mansion. It is recalled that Ginny was an excellent cook whose specialty was butter pound cake.

At one point, Sealy believed there might be oil deposits under Spring Creek. Therefore, sometime after World War II, he had geologists come down and do a survey seeking the most likely areas to drill. Several places on the southwest side of the Sealy plantation were chosen as well as several sites located in the water. One well in Spring Creek near the manor house penetrated into the clay bottom so deeply that salt water was tapped and mixed with the fresh water. This well had to be capped off, but it was done with a cast iron cap. The corrosive power of the salt water eventually ate its way through the metal and once again salt water seeps into fresh water. This area can be found because it is marked by an abundance of the best mullet in the area.

James Robert Sealy passed away on May 4th, 1962, at an old age. He is buried in Greenwood Cemetery in Panama City, Florida.

CHARIOTS OF FIRE - THE STEAMBOATS

Let's Ride The Love Boat

It is all about rhythm. The gentle sway of the deck, the whoosh, whoosh of the paddle, the kurchuck, kurchuck of the engine, all working in cadence, propelling the steamboat ever forward on her journey. The paddle wheel slices and splashes water in a rhythm, taking the boat toward its destination.

What romance! What mystery! A steamboat was full of dreams, alive with people yelling back and forth, bells ringing, roustabouts singing as they loaded on the cargo. People everywhere. Hushed conversations behind closed doors. Who is on board? Where are they going? What is driving them on this colorful, wild odyssey? What lies ahead down river?

At these times, from the 1830s, until the 1930s, the steamboat was the major link with the outside world and remained just that until the railroad came to our area.

However, when our county was being settled, it was around 1838 and there were no railroads and the stage coach lines were few. Therefore, the steamboat ruled here in the heart of this country.

These rivers were alive with the pulse of the era. The sight of one of these impressive boats working on the river was awesome. Many people watched the sky for the telltale sign of smoke and listened carefully for the whistle. Then, when they knew the boat was coming by, they would run to the river's edge to watch the steamer and wave to the crew.

The skills of the captains were tested as these large ships made their way around tight corners on the water and on up to landings sprinkled along the banks of the rivers and Spring Creek. In some places, they filled the whole river with their size and wonder.

The typical trip would be to go from Bainbridge down the Flint, then up Spring Creek the four miles to what was then known as Oil Still Springs. Typical cargo on this trip would be turpentine from the stills in the area or cotton and peanuts from the local farmer's fields.

However, there was no typical steamboat. They varied in tonnage and length. Some were a single deck. Others were several decks high in addition to the pilot houses. Some were side wheelers and some were sternwheelers. However, they did have one thing in common, they were powered by steam boilers in which water was heated by wood or coal.

Equipped with these large boilers, they sent up great quantities of black smoke from tall stacks. For miles, the smoke would be visible above the trees.

With a few exceptions, the steamboat's whistle was a deep throated sound that shook the trees and vibrated the ground. There was no unnoticed entry. They could be heard for miles.

The lower decks always carried the freight. Mostly this was cotton, corn and peanuts from the local plantations. On the return trip, there were farm implements and hardware for the settlements along the river.

True these early steamboats were not the Love Boat, but they weren't that bad either. The upper decks housed plainly furnished cabins designed mainly for sleeping. These were usually located in the center of the boat and situated so each had an outside view. As on today's cruise ships, these rooms were generally small.

When the Indian threat in our area was gone, passenger travel increased. The steamship lines began to try to woo passengers by making dining rooms as classy as they could. It was in the middle of the staterooms, oval in shape and most were shiny wood and crystal. There also were linen table cloths and white coated servants who served quality meals. This worked and the most elegant dining rooms were the talk of the town.

Life on the wharves was also a rhythm. Roustabouts worked and created a cadence as they loaded the boats. In time with their music, they rolled kegs along the gangplanks and then spun them onto the deck. People liked to watch them and some were so adept at what they did that they could make their barrels "do tricks" by spinning and popping them upwards.

When the steamboat arrived at the landing, it was a social event. Young, old, rich, poor, male, female, it attracted everyone. Ladies wore their finest dresses and businessmen in tailed coats joined youngsters and laborers to greet the boat.

Most times a horse drawn flat wagon met the arrival. It had long seats on each side and could accommodate quite a few passengers and cargo. It moved from the dock to an area where passengers could be met and supplies taken to their designation. Some wagons had canvas tops to protect the passengers and cargo in bad weather.

However, we can't forget that steamboats were a business and they had to make a profit. Owners would paint a line across the hull from bow to stern. When enough cargo was loaded on board to put this line in the water the boat was full enough to make a profit.

A great pride to owners was having their name painted on the side. Some boats had a long life and their names were always recognized. However, the life expectancy of the steamboat was not long. Dangers included accidents with rocks and stumps and the ever present danger of fire and explosion. Consequently, our rivers are scattered with remains from steamboats.

There also was the unpredictability of the rivers. At this time, the rivers flowed untamed by dams. At times, they were so high that the steamboat could not go under bridges or when it docked, it was setting up above the wharf. Then there were low water days when it would get hung up on a bar on the bottom and had to remain so until the water rose and so would the steamboat.

Traveling on the rivers in the early 1800s, was not only hazardous, sometimes it was down right scary. Trouble seemed to jumped off the river's banks and float all around the craft. Too low water or too high water was common because there was no way to control the temperamental waters. Logs, snags, and sand bars sprang up in the paddle wheel's way as the river tried to preserve her privacy. Along with these problems, the boats were a danger to themselves with fire the primary one.

Places called Bloody Bluffs as well as Murder Point, and Battle Bend were common and some places lived up to their names. Despite the dangers, settlers began using the rivers commercially as early as the 1820s. They transported crops up to the north and picked up manufactured goods in return.

Keels boats, pole boats, bateaus and steamboats were used to carry freight from Columbus, Georgia, on down the Chattahoochee River, then on to the Gulf of Mexico. If they could, they would return against the current carrying their cargo upstream. In the days before steam engines were used, it was possible that a boat could not return for quite some time. Shippers tried to remedy this by placing fall lines in strategic areas. These would be used by sailors to pull themselves along upstream.

Also in the 1820s, the Indians became less of a threat to the settlers. It was then that the Georgia and Florida legislatures enacted laws that would improve the use of the rivers to attract more settlers to the area. The Army Corps. of Engineers also helped. They had commissioned boats to take care of snags and other obstacles. They also dredged the rivers. As conditions improved steamboats made their way onto these water highways.

Around 1825, most of the fighting with the Indians in Georgia came to an end and people came to settle along the rivers. As early as 1826, the need for river improvements became apparent. Traffic was increasing as were the incidents of snags and running aground on sand bars. The waterways were now looked upon as the chief way of transportation. The steamboat was beginning to become popular.

In the year 1827, was also the time that treaties were signed with the Indians so more and more people came and established towns. In 1830, the Army Corps. of Engineers began dredging operations and also enlisted a fleet of tow boats to keep the steamboats running on the rivers.

The First Steamboats On The Rivers

In the days before railroads came into being, the natural waterways were the principal means of transporting goods. The lush crops of the South and the machinery of the North were traded and delivered by water routes.

Pole boats, bateaux and paddleboats would carry freight down stream and if they could, they would bring a cargo back up stream. Mostly, these boats worked the rivers before the days of the steamboat.

Even after the railroads came into existence, waterways were still the primary means of moving people and goods. This remained so until the railroads became more reliable and they established themselves as the number one means of transportation. However, while the rivers reigned, the railroads were just connecting links between waterways and their steamboats.

Ports were usually located in areas that had access to deep water. The main waterway would have access to other ports, putting together a productive network of commerce.

In our area, it was the Flint and Chattahoochee Rivers that flow together to form the Apalachicola, which in turn connected all to the Gulf of Mexico. On an average, it would take people three days or so to ascend the Apalachicola and the Chattahoochee Rivers up to Columbus, Georgia.

Early days on our rivers were not for the faint of heart. Men and boats had many dangerous obstacle to face upon traveling from port to port. Fire, drowning, Indians and snags all were just a part of river life.

In the old South, most trade centers were towns built at the head of the rivers. This is where farmers and cattlemen brought their crops and animals for shipment elsewhere, and it was there that they picked up their needed supplies. It was a great convenience to be able to buy and sell at the same port.

One very early steamboat that faithfully braved the wild and untamed water system was the *Fanny*. Perhaps the first to have a regular schedule, she was small but stout of heart.

The first trip recorded was from Pennsylvania to the Apalachicola River, then on up to Fort Gaines, Georgia, on the Chattahoochee River.

The *Fanny* was built in New York City, in 1823. She was 89 feet long and 18 feet wide with a cargo hold almost 8 feet deep. She weighed 88 tons. She had one deck, no masts and a square stern with a rounded bow. Originally, she was built with a mast but about six months after her launch, she was altered to be strictly a steamboat.

Mainly, stories of her voyages were a collection of tales of snags, Indians, fallen trees and too high or too law water. A memorable record tells of a huge obstruction. Fallen trees had covered the water of the Apalachicola River from one side to the other. This tangle of limbs collected other vegetation which then wove itself into a mattress of green trash. The *Fanny's* crew took several days to cut a 20 foot wide path through it so the *Fanny* could proceed to her destination.

Normally, on a daily basis, the crew of the *Fanny* cut paths through masses of vegetation, loaded and unloaded cargo and skillfully maneuvered up and down the rivers. As it the rule of the sea, she also helped other vessels when and if she saw one.

She was bought and sold many times before 1826. This is when the *Fanny* found herself in Mobile, Alabama. Her records indicate that she came to Bainbridge in 1827, where many local people gathered to greet her. On January 28,1828, the *Fanny* was the first steamboat to dock at Columbus, Georgia, thus ushering in a new era in navigation.

Unfortunately, sometime later during her trip downstream, she suddenly blew up south of Columbus on what was afterward called the *Fanny* Sand Bar. The boilers blew in a shower of clanking iron. Black smoke mingled with red smoke as the heat from the fire caused the river to foam. Fortunately, no one died in the tragedy.

The mystery of the *Fanny* is that ship records show that in 1829, she was once again in Columbus. Then, she went down the Apalachicola River. Her records state that she was used only for towing and clearing passages. The *Fanny* was officially abandoned in 1830.

The second boat recorded on our river system was the *Steubenville*. She had been running though the gulf waters for four years. Then she was assigned a trip up the Apalachicola River and then onto the Chattahoochee River in 1827.

A paddle wheeler, the *Steubenville* was built in Steubenville, Ohio, in 1823. She weighed 148 tons and was 117 feet long and 18 feet wide with a draft of seven feet. She had one deck in the stern. She could carry 700 bales of cotton or 1100 barrels of flour.

Praise was heaped upon the *Steubenville* after she completed her first trip in only four days. Her total run was from Fort Gaines on the Chattahoochee to Mobile Bay, in Alabama. Then she went on up to Fort Mitchell near Columbus, Georgia. She reached Columbus on Feb. 6, 1828. Making the total run a record of only 86 hours. This was very efficient at this time of uncertain water depths, snags and attacks.

However, not all of the *Steubenville's* excursions went so well. The following spring a pleasure excursion was planned to go 10 miles downstream from Columbus to Woolfolk's Mound, now a part of Fort Benning. Then she was to go back up to Columbus.

With the spring rains and the water run offs, the *Steubenville* had a very difficult time going back against the current. Progress was extremely slow and many of the passengers became impatient. They got off the boat and walked to Columbus. When the boat did finally come in, it was at daybreak. To announce its arrival, it fired a signal gun as much as to say, "See, I did return!"

The spring of 1822, saw the two masted brig *William and Jane* bring 266 bales of cotton to New York. This is the first recorded cotton export from our area.

The *Apalacha Packet* was another early sailing vessel. She was small, only 29 tons, with a length of 40 feet. She was 14 feet wide and took a draft of 6 feet. A schooner constructed in Apalachicola Bay in 1825, she had one deck and two masts. What happened to her after 1826 is unknown.

An early pole boat was known as the *Rob Roy*. She ran in 1828. The *Rob Roy* was mainly used to carry groceries. This is all that is known about her.

Another steamboat of this early era was the *Virginia*. She was 123 tons with a length of 114 feet, 19 ½ feet wide and a 6 foot draft. She was built in 1826, in Cincinnati, Ohio.

The *Virginia* was described as being handsome and well built. Her engine had 60 horsepower which gave her the power to run 100 miles a day and she could go upstream fairly easily. She had one deck, a square stern, and a hurricane house on the main deck.

The *Virginia* arrived in Columbus, Georgia, in May of 1829. However, not much more is known about her. It is believed the *Virginia* was retired in 1844.

Despite all of the improvements in boats and waterways, the rivers remained a wild frontier for many years to come.

Ship Of Death - *The Janie Rae*

Many sailors who rode the rivers were very superstitious. It just goes with the job, for going out onto the rivers was one of the most hazardous vocations that a man could engage in. There were many circumstances in which a man could lose his life. I imagine that river men wanted to have some type of edge up on what may be bad luck.

However, not only the river men could experience a time of bad fortune, a ship could also. Mostly, it was believed that a ship could be haunted by demons. Take, for instance, the steamboats, *Janie Rae* and the *Three States*. *Janie Rae* started out like a normal steamboat but somehow her aura changed. The *Three States* once belonged to a company in Bainbridge. However, she too, turned into a ship that no one wanted to crew.

First, let us examine the fate of the *Janie Rae*. Her problems started when she took the place of two ships which had gone down within two days of each other, one with casualties.

The swing to bad luck started in 1897. It proved to be a costly year for the Independent Ship Line. Two ships, the *City of Columbus* and the *J.F.C. Griggs,* saw their demise with both sinking when they hit a snag.

The *City of Columbus* was lost around midnight on March 30[th,] Innocently enough, the steamboat was going from Apalachicola in Florida, on up the Chattahoochee River delivering the mail. The ship was about two miles above Gordon, Alabama, when it hit a snag and went down. Luckily, no lives were lost in this sinking.

Two days later, the *J.F.C. Griggs,* sank on the Chattahoochee at Barnett's Landing at 9:30 in the evening. Along with loosing the ship in this accident, three of the crew men perished. Eugene Waterbury, the chief engineer and two deck hands were killed when the *Griggs* struck a log which was embedded in the river bed. With the vessel traveling at full speed when it hit this obstruction, the impact caused the log to be driven right through the hull and up into the upper deck.

Engineer Waterbury was last seen in water up to his waist furiously bailing out the sinking ship. His wife was a passenger on board and was saved along with a large number of other passengers. Two deck hands were helping others off of the boat when they too, disappeared into the muddy waters of the Chattahoochee River.

After the wreck of the *Griggs*, Captains William Gaines and Walter Pryor worked at the scene of the accident to remove the machinery. Later, they came back at low water and tried to recover the hull.

To fill this large gap in the Independent Line's service, a replacement vessel, the *Janie Rae*, was purchased. She was built in Jefferson, Indiana. This vessel was a 118 ton sternwheeler. Her measurements were: 110 feet long, 25.9 feet wide and needed a water depth of 3 feet to float. She also sported 12 passenger cabins.

As part of her duties, the *Janie Rae* would be carrying the mail like the two vessels she replaced. She also was no stranger to Bainbridge as this was one of her scheduled stops.

The *Janie Rae* had a rather short but violent career with even the possibility of carrying a murderer on board. This event started when Thomas Broadway, a Calhoun County, Florida, logger, took a trip on the *Janie Rae*. He was a deck passenger who was going on down the Apalachicola River looking for work.

His first scheduled stop was at Blountstown, Florida. When the steamboat neared this landing, Thomas was awakened by a deck hand. Thomas was seen by this deck hand and then he just vanished. It was believed that Thomas either walked, fell or was pushed over board.

When this was reported to the Captain, the steamboat pulled over to a bank and stopped. The crew men then searched the river for the logger. Every effort was made to find him but to no avail. This took place two days before the *Janie Rae's* demise.

A few days later, the steamboat, *Naiad*, was working her way on down the Apalachicola River when it found Broadway's body floating just ahead. Her crew retrieved the body. Thomas Broadway was then buried along the banks of the river. This was the customary way of internment as many others that were lost were given a similar burial. Makes you wonder how many people had their final resting place on the banks of our rivers.

Two days later, on May 26th, the *Janie Rae* sank at Blountstown Bend. She had struck a snag but no one noticed this. She sank at her dock. Fortunately, without another loss of life.

Their best running boat gone, the Independent Line hired a crew from Apalachicola to retrieve what remains from the *Janie Rae* that they could. The water had gone down and she was now resting in five feet of water. However, to get to the precious machinery, they had to burn her cabins and upper decks.

The men who crewed aboard her felt this was a good thing for the fire would purge the boat of the devil which was stalking her for these men felt that the *Janie Rae* had gotten the hole in the hull because she had struck the logger who lost his life just some 48 hours before.

By mid-June, the Independent Line had replaced the *Janie Rae* with a new, light draft steamboat named the *Three States*. This new boat would receive the transplanted organs: boiler, the boiler piping and engine, from the *Janie Rae*.

A Dangerous Boat - *The Three States*

The *Three States*, once belonged to the Bainbridge Navigation Company. It was constructed from the remains of another steamboat, the *Janie Rae*. This was not an odd occurrence. In fact, it happened frequently. However, the *Three States* seemed to have inherited the tendencies to be a hard luck ship from its organ donor. The crew called the *Janie Rae*, a "haunted ship" and now, also, the *Three States*.

Built in Apalachicola, Florida, the *Three States* was so named because it was built to serve Alabama, Florida, and Georgia, for coming from these states was most of its cargo and passengers.

The *Three States* had a barge shaped bottom that drew only 15 inches. Being modern before its time, it was the only boat constructed with such a shallow draft that was also comfortable enough for passengers. It had ample room for freight, and still had comfortable cabins. It also was powered by the used machinery from the *Janie Rae*.

On the *Three State's* first voyage, and after only five days, trouble was already brewing. Captain Long had found several deck hands gambling. When he ordered them to stop, they refused. He then threatened to put them off as a lesson to others who thought they did not have to listen to the captain's orders.

Being disciplined in front of the other crew members caused the gamblers to become angry. It is then that Captain Long ordered the boat to come about and return to Columbus. While the *Three States* was being turned, two of the five men jumped off. The ship's officers went after them. They seized the two and then the other three and put them in the hold of the ship.

When the *Three States* docked again in Columbus, warrants for gambling and mutiny were sworn against the five men. They were sentenced to a year on a chain gang.

Six weeks later, the *Three States* ran aground on a sand bar. This damaged its stern wheel. The captain felt that the steamboat was unable to go on and he then did something which captains are not to do, he left his ship and took a train back up to Columbus, 52 miles away. While he was gone, the crew made temporary repairs and proceeded down river without him. Better repairs were made as the vessel went along and the *Three States* made it down to Apalachicola with no other problems. The crew was encouraged because finally something went right. Unfortunately, the streak of bad luck that began the career of the *Three States* was not over.

In early 1900, it broke its shaft when it tried to steam too fast up the Chattahoochee River. The *Three States* was once again dry docked in Columbus for repairs.

With its usual unpredictability, the Chattahoochee River rose up several feet, causing the *Three States* to float high above its wharf. When the river receded, it left behind two feet of mud on the wharf and on the *Three States*. After a long delay while the steamboat was getting cleaned up, she was once again at work on the rivers.

Now you would think that this vessel's run of bad luck was over. However, it seemed only to intensify. In 1901, on a trip up river from Apalachicola, once again a deck hand either fell or was pushed over board. Crum Grant, ended up in the churning waters, in the same place where the logger disappeared that was aboard the *Janie Rae!*

The circumstances which surrounded the happening were very mysterious. It too, was as though he was pushed over to his death. The crew believed he was pushed by the previous victim.

Grant's body, like that of the logger, was not found until the *Three States* was on its return trip down the Apalachicola River. Once again, a body was buried on the banks of the river.

Later that year, 2nd Engineer Jim Wells, died on a trip up the Chattahoochee. He had contracted dysentery and by the time a doctor was available, it was too late and nothing could be done to help him. Again, a burial on the river.

As if all of those happenings weren't enough, in December of 1901, the *Three States,* while docked at Columbus, was partially destroyed by a mysterious early morning fire. The alarm went off and the fire department came. They concentrated their efforts on saving the hull. They did this by cutting a hole in the bottom of the hull so the *Three States* would settle on the river's bottom. This strategy worked.

Most people thought that the *Three States* was damaged beyond repair. Twice now the machinery had burned. However, the hull was repairable. Now, it was hard to find a crew because of her reputation. The steamship company decided to sell her and she went to the highest bidder.

Once again, the *Three States* was resurrected and then went to work on the Suwannee River. However, after a few months she returned to Columbus, Georgia. Once again she was in dire need of repair. To seemingly prove this, she sank at the wharf.

However, the *Three States* was once again revived and in 1902, she was sold to the newly formed Bainbridge Navigation Company which was located on land just above the present day Elberta Crate dock.

The company spared no expense as the *Three States'* hull was repaired and it was outfitted in style. It could now accommodate 75 passengers in comfort. There was fine furniture for the cabins as well as carpeting. Even hot and cold baths could be arranged.

She was assigned to Captain T.B. Whiteside, one of the best captains of this time. Captain Whiteside's wife served as purser on board. This was only one of very few female intrusions into the exclusively male world of the steamboat. It should also be mentioned that in the world of the seaman of this era, women were bad luck to have on board. Captain Whiteside did not get to navigate the *Three States* for very long. Tragically, he died of pneumonia. Once again, like a serial killer, the steamboat had claimed another life. She was once again sold. This time to the Georgia-Florida Navigation Company.

Here the history of the *Three States* fades into the past. She did continue to serve on the rivers of our area because there is a record of it sinking on a sandbar when it once again scraped a hole in its hull like had happened four times before.

The steamboat was repaired and became a substitute boat when one boat in the navigation company's line was being repaired. She continued serving until 1920, when it was abandoned somewhere on the Apalachicola River. Perhaps it was where the two men who "fell overboard" and drowned were buried.

Water Above- Secrets Below - *The Mascotte*

The water which slowly flows by Horseshoe Bend looks quiet and peaceful. Who would guess that there was a fight for life and cargo when the steamboat, *Mascotte* went down in the Flint River in the cold February waters.

This was the dawn of a new century. It also was the beginning of the end. Not only is the future dark and forbidding, but the death knell is about to ring for the glorious steamboat era because its days will be coming to an abrupt end. There are only about twenty five years left and then the unique sounds of the steamboat as she splashed her way up and down the rivers would be silenced. Then, these stately vessels will be gone, lost to the railroads. However, the traffic on the Flint, Chattahoochee and Apalachicola River system was still as busy as ever.

For now, conditions and business are excellent. The waters of the rivers are running high, making navigation easy. The steamboats are carrying all the freight they can pile on board. Bales of cotton, barrels of resin and turpentine as well as passengers, all are traveling up and down the river.

On November 28, 1899, the newly built vessel, *Mascotte*, left her construction site at Apalachicola, Florida. She was bound for Columbus, Georgia, carrying a large shipment of oysters for New Years Eve parties. When empty, she was then reloaded with a large cargo shipment as well as taking on her capacity in passengers to be brought to Bainbridge for the Christmas holidays. While all of this was going on, no one realized that the career of the *Mascotte* was ticking closer and closer to a quick and violent end.

The *Mascotte* was not a very heavy nor a very large steamship. She was 128 feet long and 28 feet wide and needed four and one half feet of water to lift her 123 tons so she would float.

The owner and captain was William Gaines. His half-brother, Walter Pryer and Ed Quick were also owners. William Gaines also served as the purser. Herbert Fry and H.F. Snyder were pilots.

On this fateful day in February of 1900, things were going along in a normal fashion. The crewmen shouted to each other. Deck hands crooned songs in cadence to the splash, splash of the great paddle wheel as it tossed water flumes high in the air causing the Flint to foam and boil in its wake. She passed by dark, rich forests of pines and cypress trees whose feet were wet as they gripped the Flint's red clay bottom.

The *Mascotte* was about six miles below her Bainbridge destination, rounding Big Horseshoe Bend when she met her fate in the form of a cypress stump. It gashed her wooden hull on the starboard side up near the bow. She then began to fill with cold river water.

Captain Gaines felt the weight of his responsibility to the passengers and the cargo which depended on him. Thinking quickly, he telegraphed the steam vessel, *Bessie Clary* to come to their assistance.

As the *Mascotte* sank, passengers scrambled into life boats. Ignoring the cold water, some swam to the safety of the river's banks. Bales of cotton, tubs of turpentine, slipped beneath the red brown water. Luckily, most of the cargo was secured. Later, it would be reloaded onto the *Bessie Clary* which then would deliver it to its destination in Bainbridge.

Damage to the boat was fatal and she settled easily on her side, under 10 feet of water onto the silt bottom of the Flint. *Mascotte* had the dubious distinction of being the first vessel to sink in the new century.

Several attempts were made to raise her, but she tenaciously clung to her watery grave. However, some of her machinery was salvaged and used in other steamboats.

Now the vibrating echo of the steamboat's whistle no linger bounces off the thick foliage growing on the broad banks of the Flint. The water over her is considerably deeper being around twenty feet. Even so, fishermen in the area report a mysterious tugging on their lines. The water will suddenly move and swirl as in a whirlpool. There are creaking sounds and something like a human, moaning with pain. Can it be that the *Mascotte* has left behind a haunted legacy?

A Treasure Hunter's Dream - *The Mary*

The history of the steamboat and that of all our rivers and creeks are intertwined. Each has shaped our past in one manner or another for at one time, each boat had passed this way.

In the early 1900s, the steamboat was in its heyday. Vessels were carrying cargo in large amounts and passengers in great numbers. The need for cargo even had the steamboats pulling barges. All who worked on the rivers were sharing in these good times. Taking part in this bustling business was the McDaniel family and the riverboat, *Mary*.

The *Mary* was built in 1907, in Geneva, Alabama. It was 100 feet long and 19 feet wide, topped the scales at 52 tons and in order to navigate with peak performance required a crew of eight.

The owners of the *Mary* were the Ford family with the McDaniel's son, Poley, being the captain on the *Mary*. Poley learned the steamboat business by working at his father's side. He became a very knowledgeable river man. When he was only twenty, he passed all the exams and received his Master Pilot License.

He then started working in entry jobs for he had to prove himself to the other captains. He was a full time cook and cabin boy. He worked hard and was an excellent worker. Eventually, Poley earned the respect of his fellow captains and took over as captain on the *Mary*.

Captain Poley always realized how treacherous the rivers could be and that there was little room for error. In his experience, the trickiest river to navigate was the Chipola. It was riddled with stumps and plagued with turns. However, Poley paid close attention to what the river was up to and eventually he knew where every stump was, even in the dark.

Sometimes inanimate objects take on lives of their own. So it was with Captain Poley and the *Mary*. They had become "friends" for the steamboat had seen him through many hard times. They rescued other steamboats and barges during floods on the rivers. They went through water spouts together and came out undamaged. They were inseparable. However, as it was with all steamboats, its days were numbered.

Soon after World War I, the *Mary* was traveling on the Apalachicola River when it hit a snag and tore open the hull. It sank near Estiffanulga, which is by Bristol, Florida. However, the sinking was a little bit different from that of other steamboats in that it was rumored to be carrying one hundred barrels of whiskey. This sunken treasure was much sought after, especially during prohibition. Thus, the *Mary* did not rest peacefully in her watery grave.

Stories tell us that people from as far away as Chicago came to salvage the whiskey which was to have been on board. Some even built a cofferdam to get the water away from the sunken boat. However, this did not work and the iron smoke stack from the *Mary* stayed in the water. It seemed to dare those who wanted the prize to come and get it, if they could. The *Mary's* cargo has evaded all efforts to retrieve it from the river bottom for decades.

One legend tells of a resident of Chattahoochee, Florida, who spent considerable time and money trying to bring up the whiskey but was only able to secure a tin of shoe polish.

The remains are no longer visible but who knows what still lies beneath the swirling waters.

Graveyard Of Ships - The Victory Bridge

The life of a steamboat was a precarious one. Some existed for a very long time. Some had no life at all. Several steamboats met their end in a close proximity of each other, right by the Victory Bridge in Chattahoochee, Florida. This is the span that makes it possible for Florida State Route 90 to cross the Apalachicola River, just a few hundred feet below the Woodruff Dam.

Some of these wrecks can still be seen at low water times. One of these is the *Barbara Hunt*. She was built in 1929, at Osage City, Missouri. Meant to be a tow boat, she was a heavyweight vessel coming in at 100 tons. The size was also very substantial as she was 100 feet long and 22 feet wide. She needed four feet of water to float. Also, the engine was very powerful for this time, at 137 horsepower.

The *Barbara Hunt* started service by running the Mississippi River near St. Louis, Missouri. Here she served as a towboat, hauling barges down from St. Louis to New Orleans, Louisiana.

At the end of the 1930s, the *Barbara Hunt* came to work on the rivers of our area. The hull touched all three rivers as she happily ran from Apalachicola, Florida, up the Apalachicola River to the Chattahoochee River. Then, she continued on up to Columbus, Georgia, on down river to the place where the Flint and Chattahoochee Rivers and Spring Creek met. From here, it was up the Flint to Bainbridge. Sometimes she took along barges. Other times, she was alone, doing her job.

However, the *Barbara Hunt* didn't work here long before it was bought in 1940, by the Florida Gravel Company. They tied her up to the west bank of the Apalachicola River, just below the Victory Bridge, across from River Landing Park.

It seemed as if she was then forgotten because she never moved from this spot. The *Barbara Hunt's* active, useful life had come to an end. Even though she had plenty of spark left, she slowly decayed. She lost all heart and feeling. The powerful engine became corroded and never fired again. The wiring rotted. The powerful hull rusted as it became numb in this inactive, sad state. Giving up, the *Barbara Hunt* sank where she was moored.

The *Barbara Hunt* lies in the same place today. Most of her hull is still intact under the river water and when the level is low, you can still see her.

Another casualty at the Victory Bridge is the small tug boat, *Coca Cola Bill*. She began life down in Apalachicola, Florida, where she worked the bay area. At this time, there wasn't a bridge that crossed over the brackish water of the Apalachicola River where it joins the salt water of the Gulf of Mexico.

Coca Cola Bill's life was also active. While part of the Wing Ferry Line, she was responsible for many crossings loaded with tons of oysters. She also towed barges.

However, in 1940, the John Gorrie Bridge was built at Apalachicola, Florida, and *Bill's* services were no longer in demand. Eventually, she was purchased by the Florida Gravel Company and put to work hauling gravel and sand on barges, usually two at a time. Unlike the *Barbara Hunt, Coca Cola Bill* was kept very active. However, the demands on its power helped bring about her end.

One fateful day, she was towing two barges loaded with sand, one on each side. She was headed down river from a sandbar towards the Victory Bridge. While maneuvering around a corner, the clutch failed. This left the hapless tug at the mercy of the strong river current.

On one side, the barge was caught by the current and forced into a support piling of the bridge. This caused the tug to be squashed between the two barges. One barge turned over, dumping tons of sand and gravel into the water. In all of this, none of the crewmen were hurt.

At one time, you could see the driveshaft and some other pieces of what is remaining of the ribs of this small tug boat with a big heart from River Landing Park. Now, these remains are gone.

Then, farther down stream, the remains of the dredge boat, *Sandy,* can be found. She too, belonged to the Florida Gravel Company.

The *Sandy* was constructed from hard cypress and pine rather than steel like most dredges. This gives us reason to believe that it may have been constructed at Apalachicola. Here there were many barges and dredges made by the Cypress Lumber Company from the hard wood of the cypress and white pine trees.

The *Sandy* was long and lean, made to accommodate the dredging equipment. Not much more is known of it. The long frame and ribs used to be seen at low water but these remains are now gone.

Victim At The Victory Bridge - *J. W. Hires*

The *J. W. Hires* was a credit to the steamboat industry. She had the reputation for being dependable and always made her runs. This was in spite of the fact that it was the site of a murder, a theft, witnessed a fire twice and had several accidents.

This notorious sternwheeler was built in 1898, in Columbus, Georgia. It was 127 tons, 135 feet long and 22 feet wide and needed five feet of water to float. Upon its launching, the *J.W. Hires* was given the seal of approval by the men who inspected her saying that she was satisfactory in every way.

The captain was her namesake, J. W. Hires. The first outing was deemed a very successful trial. She went to Apalachicola in the middle of September loaded with a cargo of cotton. By the end of 1899, the *Hires* was amongst the top haulers of cotton.

The *J. W. Hires* had its first mishap while going down the Chattahoochee River on an exceptionally cold night in March. It was so dark that the pilot could not get his bearings and find the river. Consequently, he ran into a tree. This took place between Columbus and Eufaula. In this accident, half the cabin was entirely torn away. Luckily, no one was injured.

One of the worst scenarios on the water is to have a fire. This is what happened to three steamboats docked at a wharf in Columbus. The *Bay City, C. C. Owens* and the *Flint* all were reduced to a pile of ash that night. No one knows how this huge fire started.

The *J. W. Hires* became involved when the captain saw this huge blaze lighting up the sky while coming up the Chattahoochee River. The captain surmised that whatever was on fire up river had been set adrift. Wisely, he turned the large steamboat, around in the narrow river and tied it to a tree on the bank. However, the captain underestimated the fast running current. He then realized that he had to release the *Hires* and go even farther down stream. The steamboat was very fortunate in that it had narrowly gotten away from the burning wreck. The captain waited until the flames were all gone to take his boat back up river to the Columbus wharf.

Even though the *J.W. Hires* was a worker, she still was plagued by debt, for as a member of a group of steamboats, they all shared in the losses. The Independent Navigation Company solved their problem by leasing the *Hires* out to the Gulf Navigation Company.

During this time, the rivers were plagued by too much rain and high water. They combined in causing the banks and bluffs to become soft, so soft that they were falling into the river, blocking the old channels and making new ones.

Most pilots knew the old channels intimately. It was not easy for them to now run the rivers trying to make a new way. Running aground became something which was happening all the time. It slowed down the river traffic and increased accidents.

As time went on, the Independent Navigation Company could not get out of debt. They sold all of their holdings to the

Columbus Steamboat Association. This included the *J. W. Hires*, the barge and all of its fittings. This sale meant that it would be a spare boat in a job pool.

This event also effected Captain Hires. He was now without job. Records say he went to Cuba, to run another boat.

In 1900, the *Hires* was once more saved from going up in flames. The steamboat, *Three States*, was partially destroyed by an early morning blaze on December 5th. All that was saved was the hull.

At this time, the *Hires* was tied up next to the *Three States*. Once again, she was cut adrift just in time and avoided being set on fire. However, next she became a murder scene.

This took place in 1901, while docked at Columbus. It was mid-March when a deckhand, Theo Jackson, inadvertently bumped up against the engineer, T. G. Rivers while he was throwing out a line. Jackson apologized but Rivers just swore at him.

As the boat continued down river, Jackson tried to avoid Rivers until he had a chance to cool off. However, a steamboat is not a big area and jobs intersect.

On a cold night, Jackson went into the engine room to warm up. Rivers was in there at the time. He ordered Jackson out and hit him in the head with a piece of iron. This knocked Jackson to the floor.

Rivers then drew a pistol and shot at Jackson fifteen times. Jackson returned fire, shooting his rifle twice striking Rivers in the neck and cheek. Rivers fell overboard. His body was recovered several weeks later.

Jackson was put in jail. Eventually, he was found guilty and sentenced to ten years.

1903, was the year in which the *J. W. Hires* became familiar with theft. While docked, a thief came aboard. He knew where the purser kept the money. He pried open the locked drawer and stole seven hundred dollars, a large sum of money back then. This represented money from the sale of cargo and the fares from passengers. The thief or thieves were never caught. According to the steamboat records, the *J. W. Hires* was still on the water in 1911. However, it is believed that she only ran on the Apalachicola River, the Lower Flint and Chattahoochee Rivers, if she ran at all. The remains used to be visible on the east bank of the Apalachicola River near the Victory Bridge. It is believed that it is here that she was abandoned and eventually sank.

However, some other historians feel that she served as a wharf boat at what is now River Landing Park. As steamboats go, the *J. W. Hires* had a long and colorful life.

Pulse Of Progress - Ferry Landings

In the long history of our area rivers, their banks were dotted with landings, places where steamboats unloaded their cargo. These landings were shared with the many ferry boats which crossed from one side of the river to the other.

Each large plantation owner had his own landing where produce could be taken to market by boat. Most of these were merely places that were cleared along the bank and lines could be fastened to trees. Planks were often extended from the lower deck of the boats onto the land.

However, others developed true ferry landings. Huge pilings were provided to which the ferry could be tied. A large wharf was filled with roustabouts who loaded the ferry with products like pine rosin, lumber and produce. Even so, there was no protection from the elements. Everything was out in the open.

Early river ferries operated on a simple principal. They were moved by cables that ran across the river. While in the water, a pilot pulled the cable and guided it across.

One of the earliest recorded ferry crossings was one operated by John Griffin in 1818. He was given a permit to create a ferry crossing across the Flint River at the place where Fort Scott was erected. Talk of having the ferry continued until around 1821. At this time, Fort Scott became a civilian settlement.

Griffin's rates for ferry traffic were as follows: to carry a man and his horse, 12 1/2 cents; a footman, 6 1/4 cents; loaded wagon and four horses, $1; four wheel pleasure carriage, $1; a head of cattle, 3 cents; sheep, goat or hog 2 cents.

In 1859, the federal court authorized free ferries on the Flint. This is when Hutchinson Ferry, located 10 miles below

Bainbridge came into existence. Other ferries came and went, but this ferry ran for more than 130 years.

The popularity of ferries waned during the Civil War. When it ended in 1865, funds were established to build a bridge over the Flint at the Hutchinson Ferry site, but it was never acted on. Several times since, this subject has come up, but to no positive end. Wonder what happened to the funds.

In 1868, Arnett's Ferry, located one mile below the Highway 84 bridge in Bainbridge, came into existence. Felix G. Arnett had obtained exclusive ferry rights on all lands on each side of the Flint, one mile above and below the now existent Highway 84 bridge. The ferry lasted for a short while, until the bridge was built.

There were ferries on the Chattahoochee River, too, but they were not as popular. Perhaps it was the unpredictability of this river and its swift current that caused this. There were two very busy ones, one at Trail's End and one at Neal's Landing.

The one at Trail's End was owned and operated by Emanuel Turnage. He established a ferry crossing on the Chattahoochee in 1874. It was at the foot of Georgia State Route 253, then known as the Spring Creek-Bainbridge Road. The ferry, known as Turnage Ferry and Landing, went over to Jackson County, Florida, land also owned by Turnage.

At the time, the road did not end where it does now. It extended outward toward the river about 1,000 feet. Where it ended is now just a tiny island near the entrance to the Trail's End channel. Most of the road is now under the backed up waters of the Chattahoochee River.

Since there were no railroads at this time, and this was the only ferry crossing for about 20 miles, it became a major crossing point. It was from here that area farmers sent their agricultural products to the markets along the Gulf of Mexico. This is where they picked up store goods and machinery for local establishments and their own homes. Steamboats also used this landing. They too, carried supplies, mail and passengers from Columbus to Bainbridge and on down to Apalachicola.

Turnage also provided wood as fuel for steamboat traffic. Thus Turnage Ferry and Landing became regular stop. Shipping companies printed flyers with the passenger fares from Turnage Landing to other points.

In 1912, Turnage died, and his son, Daniel, continued to operate the ferry line and the landing. He did this until 1923, when he sold it to L.C.

Butler. It then became Butler's Ferry Landing. It continued for only a short time because now the railroads were taking over as the number one carrier in the area.

The other ferry on the Chattahoochee was located about 20 miles upstream at Neal's Landing. This ferry crossed near the plantation landing of the Steam Mill/Cummings Plantation where the Georgia State Route 91 bridge is now located. It provided an access to the panhandle in Florida.

In the early 1920s, Neal's Ferry and Landing was sold to E. R. Ward of Iron City who operated it until 1927, when it was replaced with the infamous swinging bridge. The bridge remained in use until 1953, when it was deemed unsafe.

While the new concrete and steel bridge was being constructed, a ferry was once again used to cross the river at this point. If you didn't use the ferry, you had to go on up to the Highway 84 bridge.

This ferry, even though constructed in fairly modern times, had several problems. It sank twice in the first four months of its existence. Then, that fall, it was the scene of two deaths. It seems that two men stayed in their vehicle and drove it on board. The car did not stop when it entered the ferry and went off into the river. Faulty brakes were blamed.

A ferry on Spring Creek was established in 1852, by Martin Harden, nephew of one of Seminole County's original settlers, also called Martin Harden. Martin's toll rates were: road wagon and team, 50 cents, rig and two horses, 37 1/2 cents; carts and team 25 cents, man and horse 12 1/2 cents and 1 cent each for cattle, hogs, sheep, and goats.

The site of this ferry was next to what is now known as Reynoldsville Landing or as locals know it, Knights Landing. After several years, Hardin sold the ferry to Mr. Rhodes. The ferry ran for about one more year and then was dismantled.

A GUIDE TO FUN ON LAKE SEMINOLE

Cruising Like A Native - Rules Of The Road

To ensure that you have perfectly marvelous time while chasing down fish on Lake Seminole, it is best to get acquainted with the area. Each section of the lake has its own special set of peculiarities. Some are riddled with stumps which are hiding secretively below the surface, while others are clear, like the path between the channel markers. There are areas that are overgrown with water weeds. When in this situation, you need to know what to do so that your motor does not overheat and become smothered by the greenery.

The secret of safe navigation amongst these obstacles is quite simple, just stay within the channel markers. However, at times finding them is a challenge in itself. With so many dead trees sticking up and stumps poking above the water, the marker poles and buoy cans are sometimes camouflaged. In these instances, it does help to know what to expect.

While out on Lake Seminole, you may feel confident and stray from within the markers. It could work out okay but outside of the channel markers is where swamp land and forests once existed. Stumps have been sighted just outside of the markers, which follow the original route of the converging Flint and Chattahoochee Rivers as well as Spring Creek.

Even out in the lake water, there are obstacles. The Indian burial mounds dating back to around 10,000 years ago as well as the earthen wall remains of several forts that existed there hundreds of years ago are not too far below the surface. At high water times, out of channel cruising may work. However, a difference of an inch or two can mean kissing a stump that can end up ruining your day.

Sometimes you will come upon very tricky turns with markers being perched very close together. Best plan of action is not to be in a hurry so that you miss a marker. Relax and enjoy the spectacular view. No need to rush.

Hydrilla and lynophalis are exotic plants that grow below the surface of the water in Lake Seminole and her surrounding area. It is a very real obstacle. Again, your best bet is still to stay in the channels for the action of boats going by helps to keep it "mowed" down.

If you find that the prop on your motor is choked with grass, just simply stop, put the motor in reverse and back the grasses off then proceed. If this doesn't work because you have accumulated so much, stop your engine, pick up the motor and clean it by hand. Then, let it back down into the water.

Knowing the rules of the road is also important when traveling on Lake Seminole. Since the best navigation is in the channels, it is inevitable that you will have to pass another craft coming toward you in the opposite direction. Also, in some places, the channels are quite narrow for two boats passing. The courtesy is to slow down to idle speed while going by. This is especially true when a larger craft is passing a smaller one because of the danger of swamping the smaller boat.

If you should cause an accident, it is like having an incident with a car in that the name and numbers on your boat are reported to the Coast Guard. Also, if you leave the scene, it is akin to hit and run.

An important rule of the road is knowing who has the right of way. First, sailboats, commercial vessels like tug boats and barges and commercial fishing vessels have the right of way over pleasure craft. Boats have the right of way over a jet ski. When it is two boats, the one on the right has the right of way. Also, stay on the right while approaching oncoming craft as it will pass you on the left. Even when you are sure you have the right of way, good safety comes by not insisting. Some people don't know the rules, so drive defensive.

When passing another boat from behind, it is your choice to go right or left. Which ever you chose, be sure to stay clear of the craft you are passing.

If you are about to cross paths with another boat, the craft on the right has the right of way. Simply, slow down to let the boat continue on, then pass over the wake behind it.

When you are traveling across the wake of another craft, make sure you can see all around. Stay far enough behind the other boat so it doesn't obstruct your view.

One more suggestion, it is a good idea to purchase a waterproof map of Lake Seminole. These are sold by all the area merchants. It will help when the cruising gets confusing. If you are new to Lake Seminole, it can get to be just that. With a little foresight, you can prepare for a situation before it occurs, thus making sure nothing ugly happens to ruin your day.

Navigation In The Channels

Finding your way around Lake Seminole and her rivers is easy once you know the secrets and get the hang of things. The best way to do this is to follow the navigational aides.

While such helpers as lighthouses, buoys, beacons, day markers, special markers and safe water markers are ones used universally, not all of these are in use on Lake Seminole and her waterways. Therefore, we will concentrate on those aids that are used locally.

Buoys are the artificial markers that are most familiar. They are found in the rivers, the lake waters and along the shores. They have distinctive colors, shapes and numbers to guide boaters along on a safe course. When used with the right charts, they help boaters find their positions.

Our rivers are marked with what is called a "side of the channel" system of buoys. The best way to travel lies between these two buoys. You can tell which side of the channel the buoy is on by its color, or its number, or its shape.

Our rivers also have buoys that mark the center of the channels. These may be passed on either side, as they mark the preferred way to go.

For Lake Seminole and the Flint and Chattahoochee Rivers, there are green markers for the left side and red markers on the right side while traveling upstream.

These markers come in several shapes. The red can be triangles mounted on poles which are secured in either the water or the river's bank. Red markers can also be buoys that are conical in shape and float in the water. This buoy is called a nun. If numbered, a nun will be even.

The green markers can be squares which, too, are mounted on poles and secured in the water or on the river's edge. Green markers can also be buoys that are cylindrical in shape and are called cans. If numbered, cans will be odd.

Seafarers use the phrase, "red on right when returning," to remind them of the correct course between the red and green buoys. It means that red buoys always mark the right or starboard side of the channel when returning to port from open sea, or going upstream on a river. The opposite also holds true. When leaving port toward sea, red buoys are left and green buoys are on the right.

On some channels, it is difficult to determine the seaward direction. On these waters you must compare the aids that you see with a nautical chart. Don't be confused by local terminology that describes the left bank and the right bank with the flow of the river. To be sure of your course, use your nautical chart.

Occasionally, along the shoreline, you will see the square green markers on poles on the left bank and the red triangles on the right side of the shore. However, you may also see green markers that are shaped like a diamond and marked with squares. This is also true of red markers. These are best water markers. They indicate that the deepest waters are on that particular side of the channel.

You will also see these shoreline markers with numbers below the colored signs. These tell you the distance from the Woodruff Dam.

Regulatory markers are another buoy found on the lakes and rivers of Georgia. They use orange markings and black lettering on a white buoy to warn of hazards and obstructions or to give directions and information. They also mark closed areas.

The restricted buoy is a white one that has an orange circle in which there is black lettering. It also has orange circling the top and bottom of this buoy. This tells of an area where there are navigational rules. No Speeding, No Fishing, No Anchoring, No Skiing and, Slow - No Wake, are the most common of these rules. They also sometimes have the restriction of no prop boats allowed in certain areas.

For boats, the prohibited sign indicates a place of danger. This marker is an orange diamond with an orange cross inside. Below this is its message in black lettering. This is a white buoy that is marked with orange circling the top and bottom. Usually, this is placed because the area is off limits to all boats. These places are swimming areas, dams and spillways.

Next is the danger buoy. This one is an orange diamond shape on a white buoy with orange circling the top and bottom. The message is in black letters inside the diamond. This warns the boater of rocks, reefs, stumps or snags. Always go with caution in these areas.

Our last buoy is the information buoy. It tells directions, distances, places where there is food or you can obtain supplies and other non-regulatory messages. This one is an orange square on a white buoy marked by orange circling the top and bottom. It's black lettered message is inside the square. On Lake Seminole, the above information is also on signs mounted on poles.

Whatever the color or message of the buoy, be sure not to pass them too closely. Sometimes the hazard that they mark is right underneath them. However, it can be to one side, too. It is just safer to give them some room.

Knowing what the markers and buoys mean is a great help to finding your way. Armed with all of this information, you are sure to have a wonderful day out on Lake Seminole.

Hot Times At The Beach

Comfortable sandals, shirts made of cool, gauzy materials that move and sway in the breezes, cooling your body, providing relief from hot, humid days, a favorite pair of shorts and a cool hair do. Ah, life in the summer! Ya gotta love it!

And, there is no better place to enjoy it than on Lake Seminole. Here, where the azure sky collides with the deep green pines, you will find a sandy beach caressed by a gentle water. You will find places to hike, where nature abounds and eases your cares and concerns. Then you can close the day with unforgettable sunsets and get ready to greet a new one with incredible sunrises.

No two days need be alike. You can boat and fish or you can nap to your heart's content. You can camp or swim or just get acquainted with the local wildlife.

If you have decided that you would love to while away the hours on a soft, sandy beach, go to Seminole State Park. It offers a white beach where sand castles can be built as high as the pines. Swimming is done in the warm and inviting waters of the state park's lagoon. There is also a very clean beach house for getting rid of the sand when the day is done.

There are plenty of sheltered picnic tables and stoves by the beach just waiting for you to set up your home away from home for the day.

The park is also rent central for the area. Here you can rent kayaks, canoes and jon boats. For this type of human powered adventure, there are plenty of leisurely channels and back waters to explore that are perfect for these types of craft. Life jackets are also available. All this can be taken care of at the park office.

There is also great hiking on the Gopher Tortoise Trail. It is wide and well-kept so that even the handicapped can enjoy nature. Scattered are interpretive signs so you won't miss anything of interest.

Seminole State Park is located off of Spring Creek Road, (Georgia State Route 253) just before the Georgia State Route 39 intersection. The entrance is just before a bridge, which is over a channel. This entrance is well marked.

Diving Into Lake Seminole

Mainly, because of the alligators, diving is not a popular sport on Lake Seminole. However, there are those who do venture down into these murky, dangerous waters donned in a wet suit, toting a scuba tank, mask and breather hoses.

The best information about diving local waterways comes from those who take care of the Woodruff Dam. These men have, on occasion, left the base of the dam and have gone out into the lake itself. They say that basically, the waters of Lake Seminole are very murky. Visibility is very poor. On occasion, you can come upon a clear spot where you can see some of the lake's fish in their natural habitat. However, divers mostly report a visibility of only a foot or two.

When these men check the dam's base, they have cameras on their helmets which send the pictures up to a screen, which is in the dam's control room. Mostly, the men dive at the very base of the structure. When checking farther up the sides or out farther than the structure itself, a robotic camera is used.

Divers regularly check the dam because the concrete gets scoured by the constant movement of water at the discharge area. When it becomes too eroded, new concrete is then added. Later, when it dries, it is checked one more time before this section is opened for use.

Divers also check the water valves at the lock, being sure that these are clear, allowing for free flowing of water in and out of the lock.

In their work, they report that the side of the dam where the Apalachicola River begins, the water is much clearer and has a limestone bottom. However, this does not exist for long. The Apalachicola then becomes as murky as the Flint and the Chattahoochee Rivers.

Besides the many species of water weeds and the hundreds of stumps that plague the bottom of Lake Seminole, there are other factors which also contributes to the murky waters. With all the runoff from the immense shoreline area along the rivers and lake, and the natural flow of the current that keeps the bottom constantly churned, it is no wonder that the water has low visibility.

However, these are not the only deterrents to going down under. There also is our local "pet", the alligator. Most divers for the dam tell of curious alligators coming toward them to investigate what they are. The divers do leave the water when this happens. Local scuba divers tell that they immediately come to the surface when an alligator decides to check on them.

When passionate divers do go down, a favorite area is in the waters of Spring Creek, just above the Spring Creek Power Dam. Here, as in other areas of Spring Creek, are many deep, clear springs. Some of these are 10 to 12 feet deep. However, there are those which are about 60 to 70 feet down. In any case, the water of these springs is the most beautiful shade of blue.

Also, in these crystal, clear waters, fish are very visible, like in an aquarium. Sometimes, they will come right up to the diver, curious about him. This is especially true of the larger fish which seem to want you to swim along with them. Most divers say that they have seen just about every species of fish in this natural state from bass to bream to the Appaloosa catfish.

As for diving in the Flint and Chattahoochee Rivers, the waters are very dangerous. With the strong current, you can be swept into situations that you really can not control. Water weeds can embrace you, tangle you so much so that getting out can be a critical problem. Unless you are an experienced diver, it is probably best not to try. If you do go down, take along a friend.

All I Ever Learned About Fishing
Came From The Bait Tank

Lake Seminole is noted for her abundance and variation of fish. However, even though there are many out there, fishing does require skills.

Some fishermen are endowed with special and sharp instincts. By following these, they know how to catch the big ones. This knowledge guides them to a honey hole. So precious is this place that they will not even tell their own Momma's where it is. However, this kind of talent is rare, or maybe even an old fisher-wife's tale.

However, there are certain sensations that are unique to the sport of fishing. When you cast out your line, you experience the excitement of competition. There is the fisherman and there is the fish. Since humans have more brain power, you are supposed to be able to out think the fish. However, the fish has the home court advantage. You must meet him on his own watery turf.

When accustomed to the brilliant sun, your eyes see the motion in the water. You pick up on clues which show you where the fish are circling. Of course, you have that super new electronic fish finder which can pick out a pop-top buried in three feet of silt.

You realize the importance of keeping your tackle box up to date with the latest fish magnet. This is your arsenal. You are armed with all of the delicacies a fish could ask for in bait. You are ready to lure him closer and closer with a flashy, fleshy minnow whose wiggle won't quit. Then there is a juicy, tasty worm. One which no self-respecting fish could turn a back fin to.

A very powerful bait in your repertoire' is the stink bait jar. It may keep everyone and everything at least 15 feet from you, but, to a hungry fish, it is a *death by chocolate* treat.

What about that latest lure? The one that looks like a chandelier from Buckingham Palace. There has to be a "girl" fish out there that wants to latch on to that piece of fish jewelry.

Next, your senses kick into high gear. Your nose picks out the telltale scent of fish bedding nearby. You ask yourself, do fish bed on moonlit nights or anytime they get the notion. Do they go to a secluded, shallow water area? Do they dine on minnows or do they eat anything that wiggles.

In any event, you are out there. You are ready and waiting for that telltale tug on your line. You have watched the osprey next to you. Perched on that old stump, he has snagged fish after fish. You know that your number has got to be close. When it comes, you are ready.

Course, sometimes our finny friends do temporarily lose their appetites and aren't biting. Maybe they have heard about all of those Nutri System ads on television or they are carb counting. When this happens, fish definitely don't bite.

Suddenly, you feel a fast but definite pull! You give a sure but gentle tug and it's hooked! You can smell the fish and hush puppies frying!

Sunsets On Lake Seminole

We all seem to get run down in the humidity of late summer. For months we have been living with the high temperatures. However, as tropical as the days can be, late summer is the optimum time for beauty in sunsets and the evening skies.

All of the water vapor that brings us the wet air also provides the necessary ingredient for the beautiful colors in the sky at day's end. Like a rainbow on steroids, these many and vivid hues dominate the heavens in the evening.

Sometimes it is so overwhelming, you actually gasp for air. One sunset is more breathtaking than the other. It is a spectacular sight, but that is not all. There is a bonus. Not only is there the enticing beauty but there is a refreshing coolness that is welcome after the scorching sun of the day.

Here, on Lake Seminole, we are blessed with the panorama of a brilliant display for there are events that fill us with awe and the sunset is one of them.

The sun will cast a glowing reddish hue that is painted on the clouds. It bounces off the warmed earth and shines upon the calm waters. Silhouetted pine trees reached out for each other's touch, almost like dancing in the shadows of the soft waning light. At this moment, you are in paradise.

While a sunrise promises a new start, a sunset promises a safe haven from the pressures of the day. Once again the sun slips silently out of sight and trillions of stars become visible.

You now can see them as well as the planets as they frolic in the early evening sky. The colors of the sunset are now blending with the moon while the clouds stroll silently past.

Each season has its own dominant constellations and summer is one of the best times for sky watching. For instance, Venus is glowing in the summer sky just after sunset. Mercury is there, too, hugging the horizon just below Venus, Saturn and Jupiter. Being large in size, they can be seen with the naked eye and even better with binoculars.

The longer you stare up at the sky, the more you will see of the Milky Way and its asteroid belt as it becomes more intense. They are like fireworks on the Fourth of July as they hurry to streak across the heavens.

For those of us who are star gazers from way back when, all of this brings back memories of bygone days. As children, we would gather to watch the spectacular view of the vivid colors of the sunset slowly change into a darkening sky. Mom and Dad pointed out the Big Dipper and the Little Dipper along with the North Star and the Milky Way.

Imagine how much fun it can be for a family to have an impromptu campfire, roast a few marshmallows and lean back in a lawn chair and enjoy the view spread out before them. Fun times and knowledge that the children won't soon forget.

In our sometimes chaotic world, sunsets bring peace. As we stare up at heaven, we are reminded that we should take some time from our busy day to stop and enjoy what God has spread before us. When you think about it, you realize that He did this so we can renew our souls and refresh our bodies. There is no better place to do this than on Lake Seminole.

LAKE SEMINOLE SERVICES

Now that you are acquainted with the whys, ways and history of the area, to help you get around Lake Seminole, and to make your stay more pleasant, I have compiled this guide. It not only tells you where all of the landings exist, it also tells where there are marine repair shops. Also, since fuel is not easily found in the Lake Seminole area, there is a listing of places where gas and diesel are available.

Gasoline and Diesel On The Water

LAKE SEMINOLE
Seminole Lodge and Marina
By boat: Near the Woodruff Dam on the left side going upstream. Channel is marked.
By vehicle: Off Florida State Route 90. Going towards Snead's Landing, you will see a short dirt road. That is the access to Seminole Lodge Marina.
Phone number: 850-593-6886
Gas

CHATTAHOOCHEE RIVER
Trail's End Resort/Butler's Ferry Landing
By boat: Mile Marker 8.8 on the right side going up stream
By vehicle: At the very southern end of Georgia State Route 253 (Spring Creek Road)

Phone number: 229-861-2000
Gas

FLINT RIVER
Wingate Lodge/Hutchinson's Ferry
By boat: Mile Marker 11.3 on the right hand side going upstream
By vehicle: Georgia State Route 97 to Georgia State Route 310 follow signs
Phone number: 229-246-0658
Gas

Bainbridge Marina
By boat: Mile Marker 26
By vehicle: Georgia State Route 253 (Spring Creek Road) to Airport Road. Follow it down to the river
Phone number: 229-246-3507
Gas and diesel

Marine Repair Shops

It happens. At some time in our boating experience, we kiss a stump and put a dent or hole in the hull of our precious water craft. Or, we are disoriented and tangled up in bales and bales of water grasses causing the engine to overheat. Now, we are faced with the problem of where to take our baby to get it made all better! This problem is worse when in a strange town and you don't know where to go.

To help you in this time of crisis, here is a list of repair shops in the Lake Seminole area to help ease your mind. Also, this will help you to salvage your precious fishing time.

Engine

DONALSONVILLE
City Motor Co. - Marine Division
210 E Second Street
Donalsonville, Georgia 39845
229-524-2942
By vehicle: Highway 84 and Georgia State Road 39 both lead to Donalsonville. Second Street is one street up from Highway 84.

Here you will find a place where they can repair all motors. Certified for Mercury, sales and service, as well as service on Evinrude, Johnson, Yamaha and others. Parts are available if you want to go that route.

Just talk to Ted or Ed for your repair work. Donalsonville is a small town, so you won't have any trouble finding City Motors.

BAINBRIDGE
Bainbridge Marine
1907 Dothan Road
Bainbridge, Georgia 39818
229-246-9547
By vehicle: Highway 84, just past the Welcome Center on the way to Donalsonville

They can repair whatever has happened. They are certified for engine repairs on Mercury, Johnson, Yamaha and Evinrude. Call or stop by.

Hull

ATTAPULGUS
R & R Boat Repair
202 Griffin Ave

Attapulgus, Georgia
229-465-2628

By vehicle: Highway 27 going toward Tallahassee, Florida. Turn right onto Business Route 27. Go into city of Attapulgus. Shop is on right hand side next to post office.

They offer any type of repair or remodeling you would like to have done to your boat. They do re-carpeting and painting as well as structural repairs to fiberglass or aluminum boats of any size.

LIST OF LANDINGS

Lake Seminole

East Bank Park
By boat: Next to the Army Corps. of Engineers dock on the Georgia side, up from the Woodruff Dam
By vehicle: Florida State Route 90 in Chattahoochee, Florida, to Booster Club Road, next to the Army Corps. of Engineers office. If you are coming from Bainbridge, go down Georgia State Route 97 (Faceville Highway) to Booster Club Road. There are signs.
Amenities: Ramp, boat dock, camping, dump station, picnic area, comfort station, drinking water, laundry, handicapped access
Phone number: 229-662-9273

By boat, there is a gradual ramp and a small dock. Just be sure to go slow and stay in line with the ramp because there are stumps in the area.

This unique camping facility is nestled on the east side of Lake Seminole up on the bluffs, right by the Woodruff Dam. The campsites carefully make their way right on down to the water's edge. Most sites are graveled or paved making them very neat and easy for you to set up your home away from home.

Picnic tables line the shoreline, giving a majestic view of the water and the Dam while dining.
Historical Note: This park overlooks the sight of an Indian attack upon Army soldiers in 1817. The Indians came off of

these banks and attacked a shallow draft keel boat with about 40 soldiers on it. There were also 7 soldier's wives on this boat who had dressed as military men for safety.

When the melee ceased only 6 men and one woman escaped. This was the beginning of a siege on Fort Scott, which is farther down the Flint River, which lasted a month.

Then in 1842, the steamboat *Chamois* ran aground here and burst her boilers while trying to get off of the sand bar. Three crew men were killed and several wounded by shrapnel from the explosion.

Also, the steamboat, *Siren*, met a fiery end in 1845, when she exploded in this area killing 10 people, mostly the crew. The boat sank immediately.

The *Thronateeska* met her fate in 1888, when fire started amid ship in her cargo of cotton. It spread rapidly. However, no lives were lost. The *Thronateeska* slowly settled on the bottom which is now just off of East Bank. The only salvage taken was the fire bricks and the ships bell as well as a safe containing 70 pieces of silver.

West Bank Overlook
By boat: Not available
By vehicle: Off of Florida State Route 90. Turn onto a paved road just after the Apalachee Corrections Center and just before the Victory Bridge that will be on the left as you approach Chattahoochee, Florida. Watch carefully. The road winds upwards. You will see a "Road Closed" sign. Turn on to the road on the left. Then go right as you go on up.
Amenities: None

There used to be a launch area here. However, recent floods have closed it down as there was extensive damage to the ramp and road. However, if you are looking for a place to park and enjoy the view of Lake Seminole, West Bank Overlook affords just that. You will be some 60 feet above the Woodruff Dam with Lake Seminole below.

Historical Note: While standing here you will be in the same place where several ancient civilizations had been discovered. The earliest one was dated to have existed some 2000 years before Christ. Other villages were dated to be around 300 years before Christ and the last, a Spanish settlement dated 1400 AD.

Also, it is believed that Spanish explorer, DeSoto, on his way across Georgia and Florida, set up a camp in this area around 1560.

Seminole Lodge and Marina

By boat: Near Woodruff Dam on the left side going upstream. Channel is marked.

By vehicle: Off Florida State Route 90. Follow signs to Snead's Landing. Before you get there, you will find the short dirt road that is the access to Seminole Lodge Marina.

Amenities: Ramp, boat docks, camping, full hook ups, comfort station, ice machine, gas, supplies and motel, marine pump-out station

Phone number: 850-593-6886

Immaculately kept grounds will greet you as you enter Seminole Lodge and Marina. A well-stocked grocery store offers snacks and drinks. If you can't go any farther, a motel with a beautiful view of Lake Seminole is available. There is also that special and rare commodity in the area, gas.

This rest stop is just about a stone's throw from the Woodruff Dam and the lock to go down the Apalachicola River. This is the last gas stop before the city of Apalachicola, 103 miles down the river. If you go down, you may want to take extra cans of gas.

Snead's Landing
By boat: Near Woodruff Dam on the left going upstream
By vehicle: Off Florida State Route 90 in Snead's, Florida. Down Legion Road
Amenities: Two ramps, two boat docks, camping, picnic area, comfort station, drinking water, swimming beach and bathhouse
Web site: www.sam.usace.army.mil/op/rec/seminole/dayuse.htm
Phone Number: 229-662-2000

When approaching by boat, just aim for the white, sandy beach. As you get closer, you will see the spacious ramps. An excellent place for a picnic, so you may want to carry your lunch and claim one of the many shaded tables for your own.

Three Rivers State Park
By boat: Close to Woodruff Dam on the left side going upstream
By vehicle: Off Florida State Route 271
Amenities: Ramp, boat dock, camping, picnic area, comfort station, drinking water, bathhouse, sanitary disposal
Web site: www.flastateparks.com

Phone number: 850-482-9006

If you are coming to the park by boat, the ramp is hard to find from the lake. You need to know where you are going and go slowly. If you have a large boat, you may not be able to go all the way into shore.

You can put a boat in here, but you will find it a little hard to maneuver on to the ramp if your boat is a larger one.

A very wild and wooded area, it is a camper's paradise. Plenty of places to explore, a small boat ramp and a nice fishing dock are highlights of this campground. Anything from tents to RV's are welcome. Add squeaky clean shower facilities and comfort station, you have everything that an outdoorsman craves when he is on an outing.

Picnic tables are scattered amongst the trees so it is easy to find a secluded area to enjoy an outdoor meal.

Johnnie Howell Launch Area

By boat: Marked by white channel markers, this landing is near the mouth of the Chattahoochee River, before Snead's Landing.

By vehicle: Off Florida State Route 90 in Snead's. Turn down River Road (Florida State Route 271). The landing is about a mile up from Three Rivers State Park.

Amenities: Ramp

This is a very nice landing with plenty of parking and an easy to maneuver concrete ramp. When launching you will be directed out to Lake Seminole near the mouth of the Chattahoochee and around some very interesting islands.

The landing is dedicated to Johnnie Howell who operated a fish camp here from 1956 to1987. However, there are no picnic tables or comfort stations.

Saunders Slough Access

By boat: Channel is marked at Mile Marker 4.0 on the right hand side going up the Chattahoochee River

By vehicle: Take County Road 39 south to the very end. Turn right onto a dirt road, Bartow Saunders Landing Road. Take this road to the end which is the Saunders Slough Landing.

Amenities: Ramp

This is a place which is great for launching when you are interested in hunting ducks in the man-made islands area or fishing in an out of the way slough. The channel is marked and is deep when the water is average or higher. When the water goes down it can be shallow.

Historical Note: Being situated in the area known as the Forks, this landing may have been close to the sight of some ancient ruins. In 1901, and again in 1946, this area was excavated by archeologists. They found that this was a very popular sight for hunting and fishing as far back as 6000 years before Christ.

On the Flint River side of the Forks, an Indian fort known as the Apalachicola Fort, was found. It existed in the early 1700s.

Evidence of Spanish missions were found that dated back to 1675. This mission was next occupied by the Cherokee Indians and was known as Kettle Pond. This was in 1724.

In the early 1900s, there was a saw mill in this area known as Whaley's Mill. This area came to the attention of archeologists because of the discovery of an old, rusty flint lock gun. While excavating, Charles Moore found prehistoric pottery shards and shell deposits and a prehistoric burial mound. This burial mound is out in Lake Seminole and is now marked off by 6 poles. This is telling us that this is sacred ground and also very shallow water for it wasn't too long ago that this mound reached up above the water. However, erosion has eaten at it and it is shrinking.

Since these discoveries, because of the water and the layers of sawdust produced by Whaley's Mill, no bones were found for in this environment they would have decayed rapidly. Therefore the human evidence of ancient life had been destroyed.

Chattahoochee River

WMA Landing
By boat: Mile Marker 7.2 on the right side going up stream
By vehicle: Just off of Georgia State Route 253 (Spring Creek Road). This landing is not open to vehicles. However, if you like to hike, you can walk down the road about a mile or so, to the landing.
Amenities: None

This access is used mainly by the Wildlife Management personnel on Lake Seminole. However, if you get caught in a storm, there is a covered boat house in which you can take refuge. There are no launch facilities here. It is quite isolated and picturesque.

Historical Note: This landing was once called Hare's Landing. Here, rising eerily out of a swamp was a large burial mound created by prehistoric Indians. Amidst out of control vegetation and a thickening fog, many human bones were found, some over 10,000 years old. Most were quite badly decayed. However, several skeletons were found close together on a bed of charcoal. The area is now under water.

Trail's End Resort/Butler's Ferry Landing
By boat: Mile Marker 8.8 on the right side going upstream
By vehicle: At the southern end of Georgia State Route 253 (Spring Creek Road)

Amenities: Ramp, boat docks, camping, cabins, picnic area, comfort station, drinking water, ice machine, bait, supplies, snack bar, restaurant

Web site: www.teresort.com

Phone number: 229-861-2000

Signs mark the entrance to the channel which leads into the marina's exotic lagoon. There is a large concrete ramp. The parking lot is spacious and very maneuverable.

All types of camping is available, from tent to trailer to RV and houseboat. The Resort has new cabins too. There is full service hook ups, electrical, water and sewage. Where ever you are, you will be treated to a spectacular view of the lagoon.

Trails End Resort also has a store which contains oil, batteries and other boating necessities. There is a serve yourself snack bar as well as other items such as bread and cold drinks to live bait and a wide assortment of tackle. They also have that rare but necessary commodity, gas.

For the members of your group who do not want to fish on a particular day, there are paddle boats available for rent. There are also pontoon boats for rent for times when unexpected guests join you and want to fish too.

There is a restaurant but call ahead for the hours.

Historical Note: Butler's Ferry once crossed the Chattahoochee River here. At first it was known as Turnage Ferry and it ran from 1874 until 1923. It was then sold to L. C. Butler who ran the ferry for a very short time because the railroads were taking over in the transportation business. In its time, it was the only ferry in this area and it was a very popular place.

The remains of the road to the ferry can be seen after the Dead End sign at the landing. However, the backed up waters of the Chattahoochee River have covered over a 1000 feet of it.

Fairchild Landing
By boat: Mile Marker 11.2 on the right side going upstream
By vehicle: Down River Road (County Road 221) to the sign
Amenities: Ramp, boat dock, picnic area, comfort station
Web site: www.sam.usace.army.mil/op/rec/seminole/dayuse.htm
Phone number 229-662-2000

By water, the access channel is a little difficult to find. A winding, unmarked waterway from the Chattahoochee River leads you to a surprise end at Treasure Lake. Once inside, you go fairly straight ahead. As you near the shore, you will see the channel marked which will lead you to a gradual cement landing with a boat dock.

If you come by vehicle you will find that the parking lot is maneuverable and the ramp is user friendly.

Under the pines are picnic tables and stoves. There is also a clean comfort station. The beauty of this park has remained pristine. It is worth the find.

Historical Notes: One of the largest prehistoric finds in this area was near this landing. It attracted the attention of the

Smithsonian Institute. Here there was evidence of extensive habitation by prehistoric Indians. It is also believed to have been the sight of a Creek Indian Village. All is now under Treasure Lake.

Parramore's Landing
By boat: Mile Marker 14.2 on the left side going upstream
By vehicle: Off Florida State Route 271, follow signs
Amenities: Two ramps, boat dock, picnic area, comfort station and drinking water
Web site: www.sam.usace.army.mil/op/rec/seminole/dayuse.htm
Phone number: 229-662-2000

As you head up the Chattahoochee River, look closely on your left. You will find the channel markers that will eventually lead you to this landing. In the lagoon, the cement ramp is at a negotiable angle whether the water is up or down. A small dock on the side makes tying up easy. There are also some abandoned covered docks from days gone by. However, the water is shallow here and docking is not recommended as the docks are in poor repair.

If you have come by vehicle, you will find that the parking lot is large and provides ample room to maneuver down the ramp.

There is a beautiful area for picnicking. Tables are on platforms in the shade or have quaint roofs. Each with a stove for barbecuing. All have a view of the channel and the tiny sloughs for restful scenery. Very clean restrooms add to your comfort.

Desser Landing
By boat: Mile Marker 15.4 on the right side going upstream
By vehicle: Down River Road (County Road 221) to sign for Desser Landing Road
Amenities: Ramp, boat dock, picnic area, comfort station
Web site: www.sam.usace.army.mil/op/red/seminole/dayuse.htm
Phone number: 229-662-2000

The waterway to this landing is not very long, but it does offer easy access to fishing on the Chattahoochee River. The cement ramp is long with a gradual drop flanked by a short pier. Very low water may present a problem here. There are picnic tables, stoves and a small comfort station. There are also several walking trails to explore.

Buena Vista Landing
By boat: Mile Marker 17.6 on the left side going upstream
By vehicle: Off Florida State Route 271, follow signs
Amenities: Ramp, boat dock

This is an excellent fishing access. The concrete ramp and dock are at the end of a short, marked channel. The ramp is of a reasonable grade and is flanked by a short pier. The water is fairly deep by the shore. However, this is not a good picnic area. It has a couple of tables hidden in the trees, but no bathroom facilities.

Neal's Landing
By boat: Mile marker 24 on the left side going upstream
By vehicle: Across the Georgia State Route 91 bridge from Georgia to Florida. Here the route number changes to Florida State Route 2. Access is just across the bridge.
Amenities: Ramp, camping, picnic area, comfort station, drinking water
Web site: www.sam.usace.army.mil/op/red/seminole/dayuse.htm
Phone number: 229-662-2000

Launching here is right on the banks of the Chattahoochee River. There is a long, gradual ramp and the water is fairly deep. There is no pier but there are several poles by the ramp where you can tie up while you park your truck and trailer. Also, there is the current of the river to contend with. It is best to have a buddy along to help when launching here.

Bathroom facilities are very clean and camping for tent and RV is available.

Historical Note: This landing is right in sight of the Georgia State Route 91 bridge. At first this was a ferry landing operated by Mr. Ward of Iron City. Then, in 1927, the ferry was replaced by the infamous Swinging Bridge. Constructed of cables and wood, it was very scary when the cars and trucks would go over because it would buckle and sway.

In 1953, it was deemed unsafe and the present bridge was built. While the construction was going on, the Swinging Bridge was replaced by a ferry. It proved to be more dangerous than the bridge as two people died here and the ferry sunk twice.

Also, there have been several steamboat wrecks here in days gone by.

Haysville Landing
By boat: Mile Marker 36.8 up river past the Highway 84 bridge
By vehicle: In Alabama, take Highway 84 over the Chattahoochee River. About a mile down, on the right hand side is Alabama State Route 95. Turn here and go down a short distance to Boat Landing Road. Turn to the left to go to the landing.
Amenities: Ramp, dock

This landing is a long steep grade down into the Chattahoochee River. There is a small dock to tie up to. The parking lot is very spacious.

This landing would be perfect for the fisherman who wanted to try a different area. Sportsmen say that it is teaming with fish.

George W. Andrews Lock and Dam Public Access
By boat: Mile marker 46.4 up river, past the Highway 84 bridge
By vehicle: Site is in Early County, south of Blakely. Take Georgia State Route 27 to County Road 200. Turn west.
Amenities: Ramp

This launching facility is an easy access, concrete ramp. Water depth does very with river heights and dam usage.

As with fishing by all dams, for some reason, fish just love to hang out there. Perhaps it is the erratic movement of the water.

Flint River

Chattahoochee Park
By boat: Mile Marker 3.3 on the right hand side going upstream
By vehicle: Georgia State Route 90 to Booster Club Road
Amenities: Two ramps, two docks, camping, picnic area, comfort station, drinking water, swimming area, bathhouse
Web site: www.sam.usace.army.mil/op/rec/seminole/dayuse.htm
Phone Number: 229-662-2000

By boat, you will see the large launching ramps. Approaches can be from anywhere. This park is divided into two sections by a channel. On each side there is additional docking. One side even has a covered dock area.

At the entrance to this channel, the water is fairly deep. However, farther down, the water gets shallow. There is a small ramp of hard earth near the end. This is ideal for small outboards, canoes or jon boat launching.

By vehicle, you will find that the parking lot is sloped but spacious. There are two concrete ramps that enter the water at a reasonable angle. Here, the water is usually deep enough for launching a good size boat.

Camping is picturesque. There are also shelter houses, stoves, running water and plenty of picnic tables in inviting shady surroundings.

This is also the sight of the highest bluff in the area, Turkey Roost Overlook. It is about a quarter mile up a gentle grade on an asphalt road. The overlook is a wooden platform that has a foot hold on the side of the high steep bank some 175 feet up. From this overlook you can see the Flint River and Spring Creek and the islands in all their wonder.

River Junction Access
By boat: Mile Marker 4.4 on the right hand side going upstream
By vehicle: Georgia State Route 90 to Booster Club Road
Amenities: Ramp, boat dock, camping, picnic area comfort station, drinking water, bathhouse
Web site: www.sam.usace.army.mil/op/rec/seminole/dayuse.htm
Phone number: 229-662-2000

The channel here is rather hard to find. It is only marked on one side, so stay to that side when approaching. A short dock is on one side of the long, rather steep concrete ramp.

Tying up here should be done carefully. At low water you may find a few rocks and a stump here and there.

When visiting the park, you are high up on the bluffs that overlook the Flint River. From these campsites, you see many of the islands between the river and Spring Creek as they unfold before you in a lush green vista.

Picnicking is also on a hillside. The park is dotted with many picnic tables hiding under the pines. The very clean comfort station and bathhouse is a walk up rather steep hill.

Wingate's Lodge/Hutchinson's Ferry

By boat: Mile Marker 11.3 on the right hand side going upstream

By vehicle: Georgia State Route 97 to Georgia State Route 310 follow signs

Amenities: Ramps, boat docks, camping, picnic area, comfort station, drinking water, ice machine, bathhouse, sanitary disposal for both camper and boat, gas, bait, tackle, boating supplies, store, cabins, restaurant

Web site: www.wingateslodge.com

Phone number: 229-246-0658

There are two ramps, one at the top of a lagoon and the other near the entrance. Both share a common waterway. Both are easy to use by boat and vehicle.

The marina is very deep and spacious. It can accommodate houseboats or Go Devils. That ever important commodity, gas, is available here.

The campground and picnic area are on a scenic arm. It is such that no matter where you camp, you will see beautiful vistas. RV's and trailers to tents, all are welcome. The campground has a small wooden dock and a few places that you can tie up a small boat for the night. Cabins with a terrific view are also available. The picnic area is shaded with ready access to a comfort station.

There is a store where you can buy anything from batteries to bread as well as cold drinks and ice cream. The restaurant is located in with the store which is open every day. However, in the off season, it is best to call ahead and check the hours on both.

Historical Note: This was once the sight of Hutchinson's Ferry, the longest running in the area. The ferry began service in 1859, and ran for more than 130 years.

Ten Mile Still/Stone Landing
By boat: Mile Marker 12.6 on the left hand side going up stream
By vehicle: Georgia State Route 253 (Spring Creek Road) to Ten Mile Still Road, then follow the signs
Amenities: Ramp, boat dock

Located at the end of a picturesque channel, this park has a small parking area and a cement ramp with wooden pier. There are no picnic tables or comfort station. However, it is so pretty that a sandwich and a drink on the boat is always welcome.

Historical Note: About a half of a mile south of this landing was where Montgomery Fields was discovered. Here archeologists excavated an ancient site which revealed extensive shell midden and pieces of pottery.

Ten Mile Still - Dirt Landing

By boat: At Mile Marker 10.2 you will enter a channel that connects the Flint River to Spring Creek

By vehicle: All the way down Georgia State Route 310 to the place close to where it ends at the Flint River. You will see a dirt road on the right. Go down to the end.

Amenities: None

Historical Note: This landing is on the channel which winds its way through the islands which once comprised Fort Scott. This was an Army post which sheltered civilians and soldiers who fought in the Seminole Indian Wars. It existed from 1817 to 1821. The fort continued to be occupied by civilians until around 1848. Also near here John Griffin ran a ferry from 1818 to around 1821. There also are records that state this area was a trading post around 1882.

At the end and on the right of this channel, where it enters into Spring Creek, was once the site of White Spring. Here by the side of this impressive spring, two small cooking pits and one large one from the prehistoric days, were excavated. These pits were on relatively high ground which overlooked the spring. Near the top, crammed into the largest pit, archeologists found what proved to be the burial of an old woman who was a slave and had the misfortune of dying during meal time. This site is now under the waters of Spring Creek.

Faceville Landing
By boat: Mile Marker 16.4 on the right hand side
By vehicle: Georgia State Route 97 to Georgia State Route 165
Amenities: Ramp, boat dock, camping, picnic area, comfort station, handicapped access
Web site: www.sam.usace.army.mil/op/rec/seminole/dayuse.htm
Phone number: 229-662-2000

Just close enough to Bainbridge to be convenient and just far enough away to be quiet and pristine. The ramp has a gentle slope and the pier is user friendly.

Campers will enjoy the back to nature surroundings as well as modern conveniences.

The picnic area is excellent, with the tables following along the shore of a secretive channel. There are comfort facilities and a shelter house.

Historical Note: This landing is near the sight of Munnerlyn Landing which was a large plantation called, the *Refuge*, which was in this area. This plantation was very active during the Civil War as it offered a peaceful place to soldiers and sailors.

Here, two prehistoric houses were unearthed. Some remains were dated back to about 8000 years ago. The many styles of pottery discovered showed that many prehistoric tribes came here and stayed a while. Also some human bones were found. They were in such a bad state of decay that it was not determined that they were human until after the bones were tested.

Horseshoe Bend Park
By boat: Mile Marker 20.7 on the left hand side going upstream
By vehicle: Georgia State Route 97 to Georgia State Route 133
Amenities: Ramp, boat dock

At the end of a marked channel, this tiny landing abounds with wildlife. Seems there is always a deer or some playful raccoons around.

The ramp here is steep and the dock short. However, the water is always deep enough to accommodate a large boat.

No formal picnic area or facilities, it is mainly for launching.

Historical Note: This landing is near where the steamboat, *Mascotti*, hit a cypress stump and sunk slowly to the bottom of the Flint River, 10 feet below the surface. This happened in 1906. All that was salvaged was the machinery.

Hale's Landing

By boat: Mile Marker 20.7 on the left hand side going upstream
By vehicle: Ten Mile Still Road, follow the signs
Amenities: Ramp, boat dock, camping. picnic area, comfort station, drinking water, handicapped access
Web site: www.sam.usace.army.mil/op/rec/seminole/dayuse.htm
Phone number: 229-662-2000

This is one of the most beautiful landings on the Flint. On one side of the park, there is a deep channel that separates the campground on the mainland from a series of intriguing islands which form part of the Flint River's shoreline. Cypress trees grow with scenic abandon along this waterway giving it a tropical aura.

If you come by boat, you will find a long marked channel off the Flint, which will escort you to this secluded park. The cement ramp is fairly long and has a good size wooden dock. The parking area is large providing for easy maneuvering.

Secluded and quiet, it also has a shaded picnic area, stoves and a shelter houses.

Historical Note: This has always been a busy, temporary place for people to gather. Archeologists determine that prehistoric hunters and fishermen used this area to camp, just like today.

Bainbridge Marina

By boat: Mile Marker 26

By vehicle: Georgia State Route 253 (Spring Creek Road) to Airport Road. Turn toward Barber Fertilizer Co. Follow road down to the river.

Amenities: Ramp, dock, covered picnic tables, comfort station, drinking water, pump out station, ice machine, laundry, gas and diesel, store

Phone number: 229-246-6336

What a great place to dock! Very convenient and chocked full of amenities. For those who decide that they want to rent a dock, there are laundry facilities too.

The store is chocked full of boating supplies and nautical clothing. You can get a cool drink and a great snack. There is an indoor eating area with a refrigerator and a microwave. On the outside is a very inviting pavilion, perfect for a picnic. Give the marina a call for more details.

Earle May Boat Basin

By boat: Mile Marker 27.7 on the right hand side going upstream

By vehicle: Georgia State Route 97, downtown Bainbridge or Highway 84 to Shotwell Street

Amenities: Ramps, boat docks, picnic area, comfort station, drinking water

Web site: www.swgrdc.org/tourism/finin/earle.htm

Phone number: 800-243-4774

This beautiful park is known for its stately mansion which houses the Chamber of Commerce.

Here there are four ramps and many floating docks that form a marina. All is housed in a protected lagoon off the Flint River. This park stretches out along the Flint in both directions. A beautiful boardwalk is all along a picturesque section of the shore line.

Cheney-Griffin Park

By boat: Up from Earle May Boat Basin about ¼ mile under the first railroad bridge and before the Highway 84 bridge

By vehicle: Take Georgia State Route 27 bypass to exit for Earle May Boat Basin. Enter park and turn right. Follow the road along the river under the by pass. Cheney-Griffin Park begins here.

Amenities: Two ramps and three docks, one quite short, picnic tables, shelter house and comfort station

These ramps are not too steep. Even though the landing is on the Flint River, because of the docks, you can launch fairly easily.

Picnic tables and shelter houses are scattered all along the river's edge providing a beautiful view while having your lunch.

There is a clean comfort station and drinking water close by.

Historical Note: This landing was the sight of Arnett's Ferry in 1868. It operated until the Highway 84 bridge was built. There also was an active steamboat dock for Bainbridge here. It was also close to the Oak City Boat Yard where several steamboats were built in the 1900s.

Big Slough Landing

By boat: A short distance down from the railroad bridge. Can be seen on the right side of the river as you go up stream. It is noticeable because of the high, sandy sides. The landing is just a short distance down the channel.

By vehicle: Down East River Road to Big Slough Landing Road which is on the left hand side.

Amenities: Ramp

This landing is somewhat shallow. Therefore, it is best used by small, shallow draft boats. However, when the water is up, anyone can use it. There is no place to tie up while you park your vehicle. However, there also is the absence of water action. A long rope which can be attached to a tree should do the trick. The ramp is short but exotic. The parking lot does not afford a lot of room in which to maneuver.

Flint River Heights Landing

By boat: Proceeding up the Flint River, past the railroad bridge, this landing is on the left hand side. You will see it because it has unique sides which look like large, rounded rock.

By vehicle: From Highway 84, turn down Georgia State Route 253 (Spring Creek Road). This will take you past Flint River Mills. Go down this road to Flint River Heights Road. It will be on your right. Take this to where it ends at Boat Landing Road. Turn to the right. It is a few hundred feet down.

Amenities: Ramp

This is a user friendly ramp. There is room to maneuver your vehicle as you launch. The gradual cement ramp leads into deep water so even when the water is down, the ramp is a good launching place for larger boats. The only draw back is that there is no where to tie up while you park and being on the river, there is water action from the current and other boaters. Best is to bring a friend.

Spring Creek

Sealy's Point

By boat: Short channel off Spring Creek channel, on the left side. Also, a long channel off of the Flint, on the left hand side, just across from River Junction Park at mile marker 4.4.

By vehicle: Off Georgia State Route 374 South

Amenities: Ramp, boat dock, picnic area, comfort station

A cozy landing with a long, gradual slope and a nice, long pier. There is also a handicap pier for fishing to the left of the ramp. Picnic tables and stoves are scattered along the banks. They offer a great view of the intriguing waters of Spring Creek.

Historical Note: The archeological digs which took place at Sealy's found that this site was used extensively by hunters and fishermen. Also, on this land once stood a huge mansion house. Now the only evidence of its existence is the tall windmill which is east of this landing.

Where the Sealy mansion once graced the shoreline, there were found quite a few pottery shards with markings dating it to somewhere around 1000 years before Christ.

Spring Creek Park

By boat: A long channel off Spring Creek. On the left side there is a sign that says, "Marina".

By vehicle: Off Georgia State Route 253 (Spring Creek Road) to Reynolds Landing Road (County Road 126) follow the signs to the end of the road

Amenities: Ramp, boat dock, picnic area, comfort station, drinking water, ice machine next door at Spring Creek Park Resort which also has 2 restaurants a motel and camping

Web site: www.sam.usace.army.mil/op/rec/seminole/dayuse.htm

Phone number: 229-662-2000

The beauty here is only outshined by the great fishing of Spring Creek. The ramp is easy to maneuver and the waters are very inviting. Picnic tables are in shady grassy areas and plenty of stoves are available.

Adjacent to the park is Spring Creek Park Resort. It has a small store and two restaurants as well as a motel and camping area.

Historical Note: This area is the site of one of the original campgrounds and motels in the area, dating back to in the 1940s.

Reynoldsville Park/Knight's Landing
By boat: Short marked channel off Spring Creek
By vehicle: Off Georgia State Route 253 (Spring Creek Road) then down a dirt road (County Road 108)
Amenities: Ramp, boat dock, picnic area, comfort station
Web site: www.sam.usace.army.mil/op/rec/seminole/dayuse.htm
Phone number: 229-662-2000

A series of channel markers will take you from Spring Creek to Reynoldsville Park Landing. Here you will find a short pier to tie up to.

The parking lot is spacious and launching is easy from the concrete ramp. The picnic tables are nestled amongst stately live oaks decorated by Spanish moss.

At one time, this park and Spring Creek Landing were connected by a paved road. Now it is closed to motorized traffic but it makes a great walking trail if you want to stretch your legs and explore a bit.

Historical Note: This was once the sight of a ferry landing known as Harden's Ferry, in the 1850s. It was later sold to Mr. Rhodes and became Rhodes Ferry.

Ralph King Landing

By boat: On right hand side of channel going up stream
By vehicle: Going down Georgia State Route 253 (Spring Creek Road) from Bainbridge, it is off of a dirt road on the left before Pace's Fish Camp. Follow signs
Amenities: Two ramps, two floating boat docks and comfort station

This picturesque landing is nestled on a red cliff bank. It has a wide, concrete ramp that sports floating metal docks on each side. The parking lot is spacious and easy to maneuver. There are no picnic tables. However, there is a bathroom facility.

Decatur Lake Landing

By boat: Up stream after the Spring Creek Power Dam, north side
By vehicle: Down Georgia State Route 253 (Spring Creek Road) when coming from Bainbridge. Just go over the bridge and you will encounter a short dirt road on the right, Decatur Landing Road.
Amenities: Ramp

This is a launching area which has been in use for many decades. The ramp is a gentle slope and the parking lot is generous.
Historical Note: While here, you will notice the picturesque yellow building to the right of the ramp. This used to be the power dam which generated electricity from 1919 to 1957, for the cities of Bainbridge, Brinson and Donalsonville.

Smith's Landing
By boat: Farther up Spring Creek than the marked channel. Use caution.

By vehicle: Down Georgia State Route 253 (Spring Creek Road). When coming from Bainbridge, turn onto the dirt road. There are signs directing you to the landing. If you go to the bridge across Spring Creek, you have passed it.

Amenities: Ramp, picnic area

This landing gives you a back to nature, wilderness feeling with its swift current and rocky banks. The picnic tables are tucked under live oaks providing for shady relaxation.

The cement ramp makes its way down at a gradual grade. Just be careful of the stumps and rocky bottom. A small boat and motor fair the best.

Bartow-Gibson Road Access
By boat: Reached best by a very small boat, like a canoe or row boat or small boat and motor

By vehicle: At the intersection of Bartow Gibson Highway and Highway 84, on the right hand side when coming from Donalsonville

Amenities: Ramp

This is an access which is best used by small boats that have a shallow draft. While it is full of stumps and the terrain is rugged, there is some very good fishing here in this quiet and untamed area of the Creek.

Fish Pond Drain

Cummings Access

By boat: First landing on left going upstream from the Dam

By vehicle: Off Georgia State Route 39 South

Amenities: Ramp, boat dock, camping, picnic area, comfort station, drinking water

Web site: www.sam.usace.army.mil/op/rec/seminole/dayuse.htm

Phone number: 229-662-2000

This is a small camping and launching area. The concrete ramp is nice and gradual with a user friendly pier for docking. RV camping as well as tent camping is welcome. Picnic tables and stoves are tucked under the pines to provide cooling shade. The comfort station is clean.

Seminole State Park

By boat: A short channel on right hand side going upstream from the Woodruff Dam

By vehicle: Off Georgia State Route 253 (Spring Creek Road) just before the intersection with Georgia State Route 39

Amenities: Ramps, docks, camping, picnic area, comfort stations, drinking water, ice machine, cabins, bath house, swimming

Web site: www.gastateparks.org
Phone number: 229-861-3137

Six boat ramps and four docks provide quick and easy boat launching no matter what the size of your craft. However, if you come by boat, you can ride in the lagoon, but there are no docking facilities.

For visitors, you can experience anything from sleeping in a fully equipped, modern cabin, complete with coffeemaker, to a cozy tent and sleeping bag under the stars. Two of the cabins have been designated pet friendly, which means you may make a reservation for the family pet to spend time at the lake with everyone.

If RV camping trailers are your idea of roughing it, you will find plenty of scenic sites with full hook ups, water and sewage and electric. If you prefer, you can go primitive. The restrooms and shower facilities are squeaky clean and inviting.

There is an enclosed sandy beach, perfect for swimming and sunbathing. For picnic lovers, there are plenty of picnic tables and grills along with group shelters.

Seminole State Park is handicapped friendly. Even their main nature trail, the Gopher Tortoise Trail, is handicapped accessible.

Ray's Lake Access
By boat: End of the Fish Pond Drain channel
By vehicle: Off Georgia State Route 374 North
Amenities: Ramp, boat dock, picnic area, comfort station, drinking water, handicapped access
Web site: www.sam.usace.army.mil/op/rec/seminole/dayuse.htm
Phone number: 229-662-2000

By boat, you turn right as you exit the Seminole State Park channel. Then proceed upstream until you come to the end. That is where you will find Ray's Lake. On the right hand side of the lake is the landing. The concrete ramp and short pier are easy to get to. A shelter house and picnic tables make this a perfect place to relax before the ride home. Bathroom facilities are available.

Turkey Pond Drain

Cypress Pond Landing
By boat: Top of Turkey Pond Drain
By vehicle: Off Georgia State Route 374 South
Amenities: Ramp, boat dock, picnic area, comfort station, drinking water
Web site: www.sam.usace.army.mil/op/rec/seminole/dayuse.htm
Phone number: 229-662-2000

A very user-friendly ramp that gives access to a very unusual channel. You can lower your boat down the long sloping concrete ramp. However, at first you will wonder, "How can I get through all those dead trees!" Upon looking closely, you will see that there are channel markers to take you through the maze.

Going left and under the bridge, the channel eventually winds its way toward Spring Creek. If you go straight, this will lead you to Lake Seminole.

One shortcoming of the park is that the parking lot is narrow and the maneuverability for putting your boat in is difficult for larger craft.

Apalachicola River

Clyde Hopkins Memorial Park and Pavilion
By boat: Lock through the Woodruff Dam. Go under the old railroad bridge and Victory Bridge. Landing is on left.
By vehicle: Georgia State Route 97 becomes Florida State Route 269 in Chattahoochee, Florida. You can also take Georgia State Route 97 to Booster Club Road, then on to

Chattahoochee, Florida. Turn down the road which is just before Hardees Restaurant. Take this road down to the park.

Amenities: Ramp, dock, picnic tables, comfort station

The ramp is cement which drops gradually to the water. It has a floating dock which is great to tie up to while you park in the spacious lot.

Picnic tables abound as do grassy meadows.

Historical Note: Perhaps it is its history, but this area has an aura of mystery about it. This was the site of an archeological find of a burial mound and a residential mound. The burial mound was under the Victory Bridge. The residential mound still exists and is noted by an historical sign. This area has been completely excavated and all of the artifacts are in the museum at the University of Florida in Tampa.

Across from this park, on the other river bank is the wreck of the steamboat, *Barbara Hunt*. At low water times, the top of the steamboat is visible as is some of what use to be the deck.

This area is also near a geological phenomenon known as a river boil. If you take your boat to just above the Victory Bridge, on the way to the Woodruff Dam, you can see it. It is about 300 yards down from the wing wall of the lock. It is visible as an area where there are constantly concentric circles in the water.